JANUARY

NEW BEGINNI

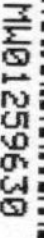

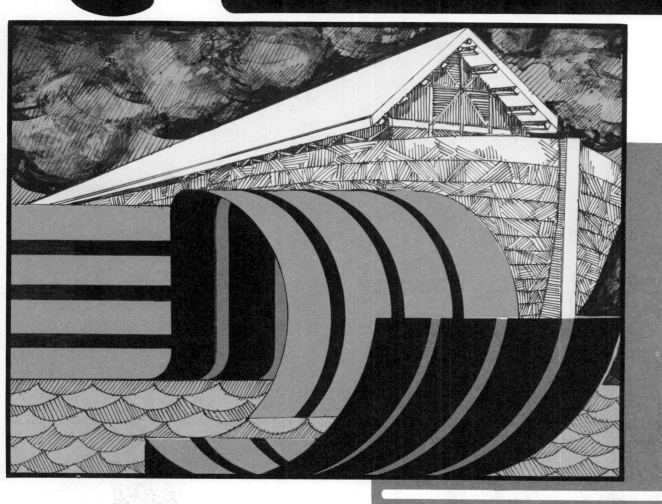

JANUARY

	1st WEEK	2nd WEEK	3rd WEEK	4th WEEK	5th WEEK
SUNDAY					
MONDAY					
TUESDAY					
WEDNESDAY					

BIRTHDATES OF PRESIDENTS/ FAMOUS PEOPLE:

Millard Fillmore
Born: Jan. 7, 1880

Richard Nixon
Born: Jan. 9, 1913

William McKinley
Born: Jan. 29, 1843

Franklin D. Roosevelt
Born: Jan. 30, 1882

Paul Revere
(Midnight rider who warned of the coming of British soldiers.)
Born: Jan. 1, 1735

Betsy Ross
(Maker of the first American flag.)
Born: Jan. 1, 1752

FLOWER:

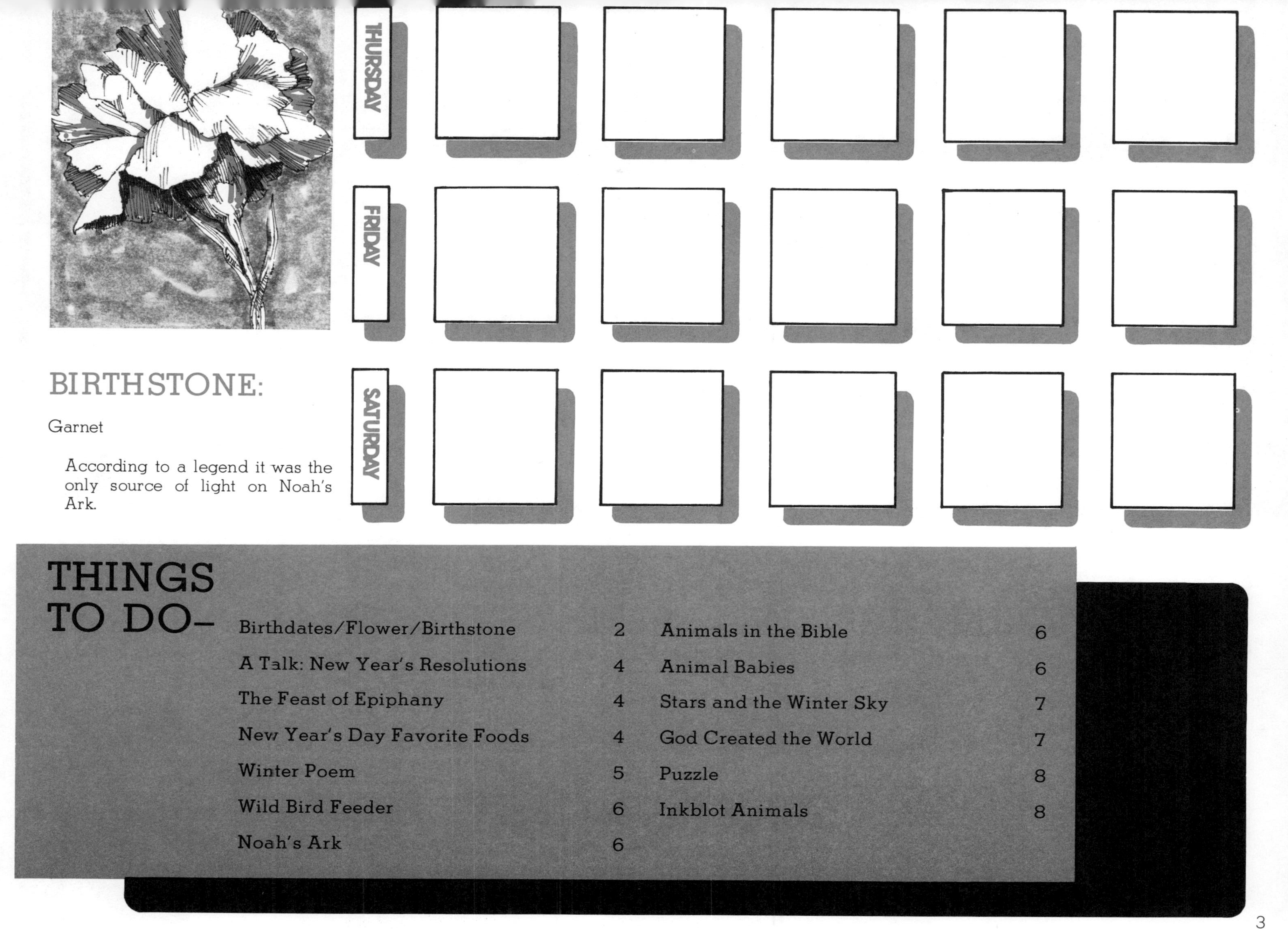

BIRTHSTONE:

Garnet

According to a legend it was the only source of light on Noah's Ark.

THINGS TO DO–

NEW BEGINNINGS

A TALK: NEW YEAR'S RESOLUTIONS

A good start at something usually promotes progress along the way, and a good ending. A New Year's resolution is an attempt to make a good start, one that we trust will lead us along a better path in our lives. A bad start, on the other hand, may make continuing difficult; it may cause discouragement and a tendency to quit our efforts too soon. The first of the year is a time for fresh beginnings and better resolutions. Try to make resolutions that are guides to Christian action.

In thinking about change—and a resolution is an attempt to change something—consider the Scripture which says:

"I can do all things through Christ which strengtheneth me."

Philippians 4:13

THE FEAST OF EPIPHANY

The eve of Jan. 6 ends the Twelve Days of Christmas, and signals the end of the Christmas or yuletide festivities. The word "Epiphany" refers to the manifestation or appearance of God in visible form. Jan. 6 is also the day we remember the visit of the Magi (or the kings) to the manger in Bethlehem. This date is commemorated in Shakespeare's play, *Twelfth Night,* which he wrote to celebrate the Christmas season.

"And the Word was made flesh, and dwelt among us (and we beheld His glory, the glory as of the only begotten of the Father) full of grace and truth."

John 1:14

NEW YEAR'S DAY FAVORITE FOODS

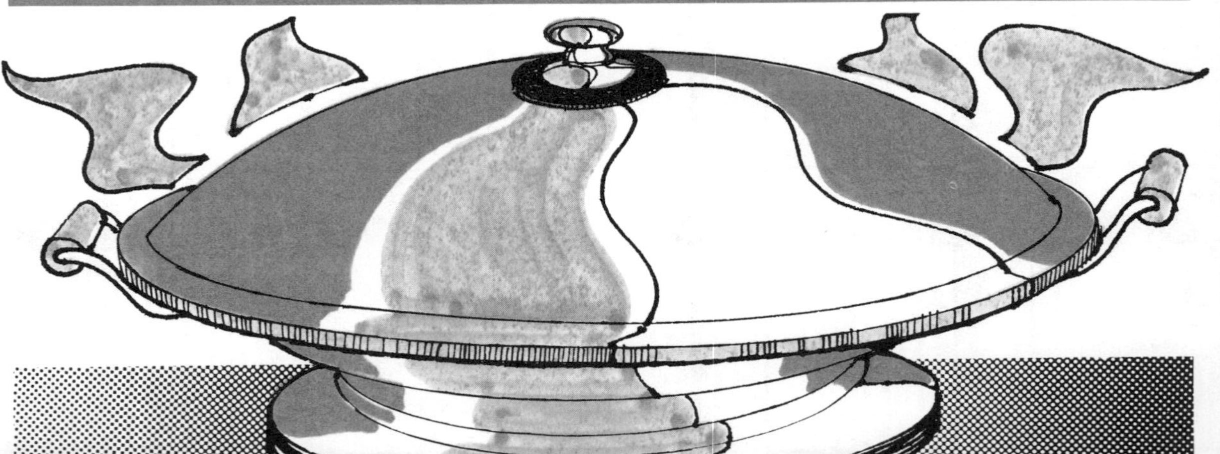

For I know that in me (that is, in my flesh) dwelleth no good thing: for to will is present in me; but how to perform that which is good I find not.

"For the good that I would I do not: but the evil which I would not, that I do.

"Now if I do that I would not, it is no more I that do it, but sin that dwelleth in me.

"I find then a law, that, when I would do good, evil is present with me.

"For I delight in the law of God after the inward man."

Romans 7:18-22

New Year's Day has its favorite foods. American Indians, for example, associated New Year's Day with salmon and acorns, and based ceremonies on the eating of these foods. Black-eyed peas were considered a great delicacy during the early days of this country, and were used to celebrate New Year's Day in the Virginia Colonies. As everyone knows, turkey has been very popular both on New Year's Day and on Christmas Day in the U.S.A. The people of Sweden eat lutfish, cream sauce, boiled potatoes, and rice pudding as their special foods at this time of the year. Many drinks are also associated with the ringing of the new year: The traditional wassail bowl is drunk from in England, and passed around, with cakes and breads, to friends. The people of Holland drank a hot, spiced beverage, and ate with it doughnuts and apple fritters. Food may portend a good year—a full salt shaker is so regarded in the far East. The people of India think only new foods are to be cooked on the first day of the year, to bring prosperity.

Things will be different in heaven:

"They shall hunger no more, neither thirst anymore; the sun shall not strike them, nor any scorching heat."

(Revelation 7:16-17)

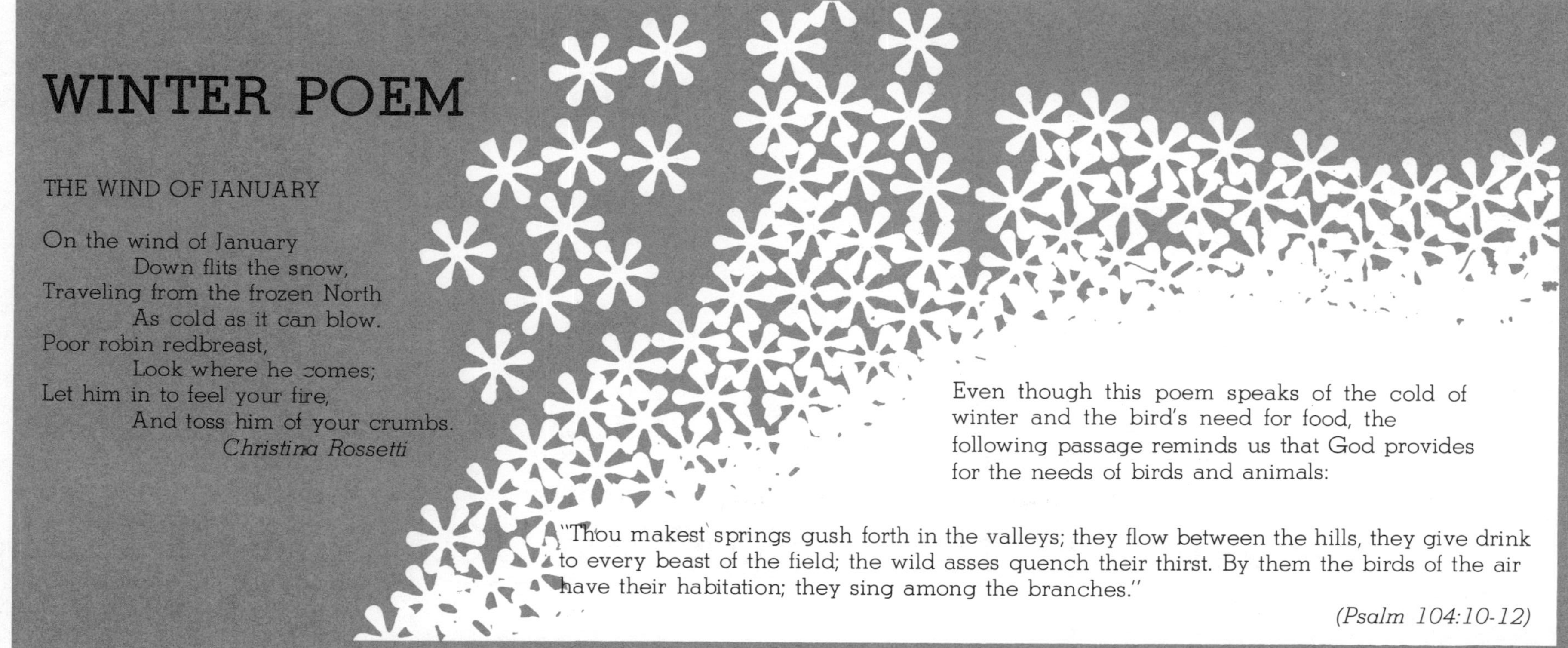

WINTER POEM

THE WIND OF JANUARY

On the wind of January
        Down flits the snow,
Traveling from the frozen North
        As cold as it can blow.
Poor robin redbreast,
        Look where he comes;
Let him in to feel your fire,
        And toss him of your crumbs.
                Christina Rossetti

Even though this poem speaks of the cold of winter and the bird's need for food, the following passage reminds us that God provides for the needs of birds and animals:

"Thou makest springs gush forth in the valleys; they flow between the hills, they give drink to every beast of the field; the wild asses quench their thirst. By them the birds of the air have their habitation; they sing among the branches."

(Psalm 104:10-12)

MAKE A WILD BIRD FEEDER FOR YOUR YARD

THINGS YOU NEED:

- heavy string/cord
- large pine cone
- spoon
- peanut butter
- bird seed
- waxed paper

HERE'S ALL YOU DO:

1. Tie the cord to the top petals of the pine cone.
2. Spoon peanut butter between the petals.
3. Place birdseed on the waxed paper.
4. Roll the pine cone in the birdseed.
5. Hang the feeder in a tree and watch the birds eat.

"Are not two sparrows sold for a farthing? And one of them shall not fall on the ground without your Father. But the very hairs of your head are all numbered. Fear ye not therefore; ye are of more value than many sparrows."

(Matthew 10:29-31)

"And God made the beast of the earth after his kind, and cattle after their kind, and everything that creepeth upon the earth after his kind: and God saw that it was good."

(Genesis 1:25)

"And out of the ground the Lord God formed every beast of the field and every fowl of the air; and brought them unto Adam to see what he would call them: and whatsoever Adam called every living creature, that was the name therefore.

"And Adam gave names to all cattle, and to the fowl of the air, and to every beast of the field."

(Genesis 2:19-20)

MAKING YOUR OWN VERSION OF NOAH'S ARK

God sent the Flood to give the human race a fresh beginning:

"And God said to Noah, 'I have determined to make an end of all flesh, for the earth is filled with violence through them; behold, I will destroy them with the earth. Make yourself an ark of gopher wood; make rooms in the ark, and cover it inside and out with pitch'" *(Genesis 4:13-14)*

SPEAKING OF ANIMALS IN THE BIBLE

Do you know what the biggest baby animal in the world is? It is a baby whale, from 14 feet to 20 feet long, weighing 8 tons (16,000 lbs.). Have you ever read the story of Jonah in the Bible? "And the Lord appointed a great fish to swallow up Jonah; and Jonah was in the belly of the fish three days and nights," *(Jonah 1:17)*.

Draw a picture of a big fish with a very small man beside it. Or use a sheet of construction paper for the whale and a smaller cutout, same paper, but different color, for Jonah. What color should the big fish be?

WHAT DO YOU CALL THE BABIES OF THE FOLLOWING ANIMALS?

cow ________ fish ________

dog ________ bird ________

cat ________ goat ________

lion ________ pig ________

Note God's instructions to Noah and make an Ark out of construction paper.

"This is how you are to make it: the length of the ark three hundred cubits, its breadth fifty cubits, and its height thirty cubits. Make a roof for the ark, and finish it to a cubit above; and set the door of the ark in its side; make it with lower, second, and third decks" *(Genesis 4:15-16).*

Let 300 cubits (length) be 12 inches; let 50 cubits (width) be 2 inches; and let 30 cubits (height) be 1½ inches. Draw the three decks and the door; or make them from construction paper of a different color; or draw them in with crayons.

STARS AND THE WINTER SKY

"January is named for Janus, a Roman god who was thought to be the doorkeeper to heaven. He had two faces, one looking at the past, one looking at the future. The key he holds unlocks the door to the New Year." Make a drawing of Janus looking forward and backward—he has two faces, one looking each way.

Many months of the calendar were named by the Romans. The Romans ruled all the peoples who lived around the Mediterranean Sea, including the Jews during the time of Christ.

Epiphany, Jan. 6, reminds us that the Wise Men followed the bright star to Bethlehem. Draw a picture of the star in the sky over Bethlehem with the Wise Men below going toward Bethlehem on their camels.

January is the month of beginnings. "In the beginning, God created the heavens and the earth" *(Genesis 1:1).*

Which of these are mentioned in the Bible? (Try using a Bible concordance for this purpose.)

The answers: cow/calf; dog/puppy; cat/kitten; lion/cub; fish/fish; bird/bird; goat/kid; pig/piglet.

GOD CREATED THE WORLD

Read the story in Genesis 1:1-31.

Get a large sheet of wrapping paper, about 15"—18" wide and as long as you need to picture light, darkness, the land, sea, firmament, plants, animals, and man. You may want a sheet of paper several feet long.

After you have mounted the long wrapping paper on the wall (or possibly laid it down on the floor), cut out smaller pieces of construction paper, using different colors. (Light: use a light paper; darkness: use dark blue or black paper; water: use light blue paper; land: use brown or green paper; vegetation: use yellow, green, and brown paper, and cut it to resemble plants, flowers, and grass; trees: use green and brown paper; living creatures: various colors for dogs, lions, whales, birds, and so on, making as many as you wish, according to the size of the paper you are using).

Or, you could begin with the large strip of wrapping paper, very light in color, and then use crayons to draw in the land, sea, firmament, animals, man, plants, and so on.

PUZZLE

See how many of the words listed below you can find in this puzzle. Look up, down, and across.

The key words are:

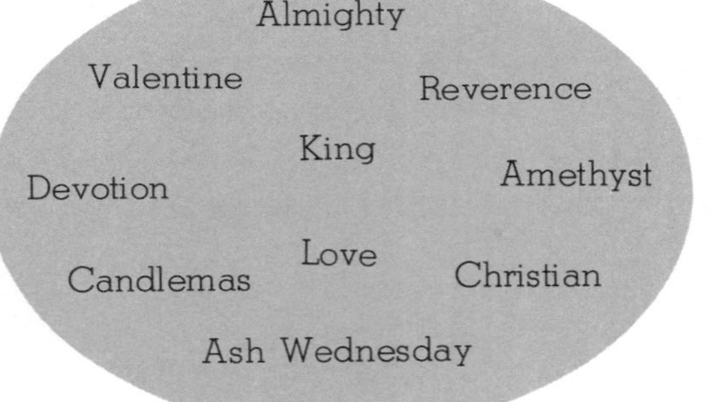


```
N V W D E V O T I O N M
A A L M I G H T Y K A B
P S O C H R I S T I A N
T A H A X K Y L L O I J
R C S W T W Y O N K B Q
E E J Q E B D U M I O Q
V G L Z T D W E I N K S
E F N T Z X N A C G D F
R H P Y O M K E L A Z A
E O A M E T H Y S T U V
N Z X W Y B P T R D J M
C C A N D L E M A S A L
F M V A L E N T I N E Y
```

INKBLOT ANIMALS

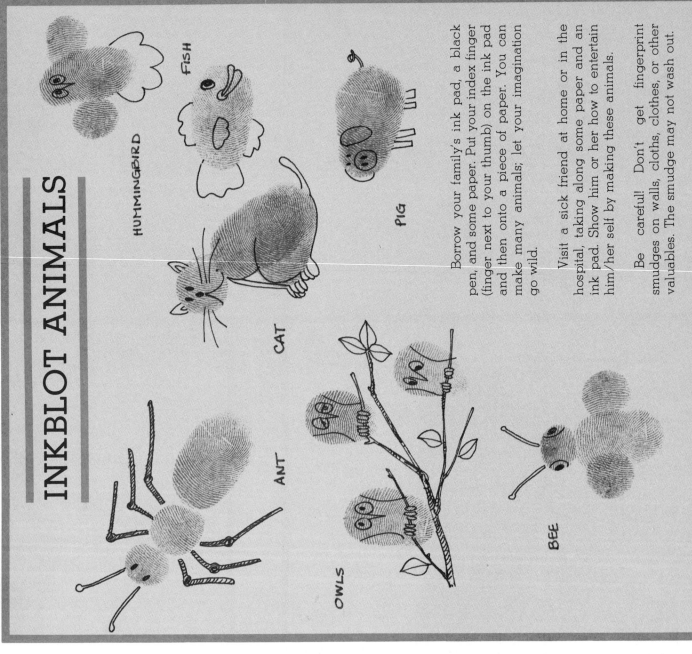

ANT

CAT

HUMMINGBIRD

FISH

OWLS

PIG

BEE

Borrow your family's ink pad, a black pen, and some paper. Put your index finger (finger next to your thumb) on the ink pad and then onto a piece of paper. You can make many animals; let your imagination go wild.

Visit a sick friend at home or in the hospital, taking along some paper and an ink pad. Show him or her how to entertain him/her self by making these animals.

Be careful! Don't get fingerprint smudges on walls, cloths, clothes, or other valuables. The smudge may not wash out.

FEBRUARY

WHAT IS SAYING NO?

FEBRUARY

	1st WEEK	2nd WEEK	3rd WEEK	4th WEEK	5th WEEK
SUNDAY					
MONDAY					
TUESDAY					
WEDNESDAY					

BIRTHSTONE:

Amethyst

A symbol of serenity.

FLOWER:

Violet

A symbol of modesty.

Both of these virtues are mentioned in Scripture: "Is not your fear of God your confidence [serenity] and the integrity of your ways your hope?"

(Job 4:6)

"What doth the Lord require of thee, but to do justly, and to love mercy, and to walk humbly [modestly] with thy God?"

(Micah 6:8)

BIRTHDATES OF PRESIDENTS/ FAMOUS PEOPLE:

Abraham Lincoln
Born: Feb. 12, 1809

George Washington
Born: Feb. 22, 1732

Julia Ward Howe
(Wrote and published the "Battle Hymn of the Republic.")
Born: Feb. 1, 1862

Thomas Edison
Born: Feb. 11, 1847

THURSDAY

FRIDAY

SATURDAY

THINGS TO DO–

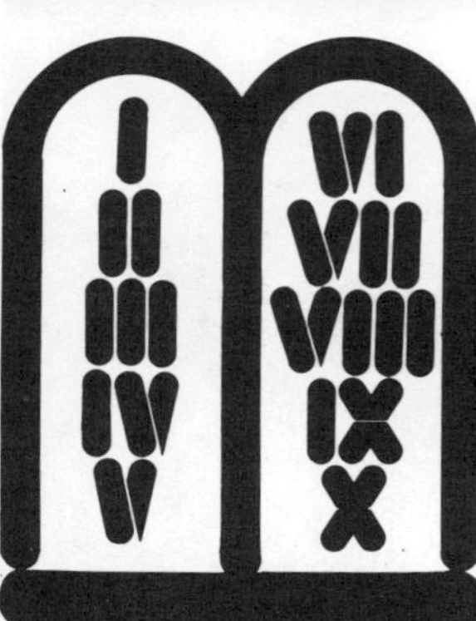

WHAT IS SAYING NO?

GOD TALKS TO US

Sinful human beings are inclined to be deceitful. The Bible says, "Deceit is in the heart of those who devise evil, but those who plan good have joy" *(Proverbs 12:20).*

Saying "no" to evil is essential in parent-child relationships. The child is often willful, not willing to heed mature advice. Parents should be guided by the following Scripture: "Train up a child in the way he should go, and when he is old he will not depart from it" *(Proverbs 22:6).*

Children need to learn the meaning of obedience as Christ did: "Although he was a Son, he learned obedience through what he suffered" *(Hebrews 5:8).*

WHAT WOULD WASHINGTON SAY TO CHILDREN TODAY?

George Washington was our first president, and some think the greatest American. He was an honest man; he always tried to do well by and for his countrymen; and he helped start this country toward its greatness. He would ask children today to be honest; to work hard; to accept but try to overcome difficulties and adversity; and to respect others. Washington was a God-revering man, and he would advise us to take our Christian faith seriously.

The theme of this month is—"What Is Saying NO"? Honesty means saying no to lies, cheating, and taking unfair advantage of others. "How forceful are honest words!" *(Job 6:25)*

WHAT WOULD LINCOLN SAY TO CHILDREN TODAY?

Abraham Lincoln was a great man, the 16th president of the United States. If he were alive today he probably would have a message for children as part of the commemoration of his birthday. What would he say? We do not know for sure, but it would probably be some wise counsel: Be kind to others (Lincoln was known for his kindness); be gentle to others (he was a gentle and patient man); and persevere toward your goals (Lincoln was a man who worked hard to realize goals). Lincoln would likely also counsel: "Be compassionate toward others who are less fortunate than you."

Think about Lincoln and the following Scriptures:

> "He who withholds kindness from a friend forsakes the fear of the Almighty."
>
> *(Job 6:14)*

> "A gentle tongue is a tree of life."
>
> *(Proverbs 15:4).*

GROUNDHOG DAY

This day falls on Feb. 2 also. Weather superstitions and predictions are associated with Groundhog Day: If the groundhog emerges from its winter sleep and observes its shadow on a clear and sunny day, it becomes frightened and returns to hibernation for another six weeks. To the farmers this meant continuing cold weather and possibly poorer crops because they would not be able to plant their grain early enough. If, however, the groundhog found dull and gray skies, this meant the cold weather would yield to spring warmth in four weeks, and crops would be planted earlier.

The Bible has many passages concerning crops and animals. "Pharoah dreamed that he was standing on the Nile, and behold, there came up out of the Nile seven cows sleek and fat, and they fed in the reed grass. And behold, seven other cows, gaunt and thin, came up out of the Nile after them, and stood by the other cows on the bank of the Nile. And the gaunt and thin cows ate up the seven sleek and fat cows. And Pharaoh awoke. And he fell asleep and dreamed a second time: and, behold, seven ears of grain, plump and good, were growing on one stalk. And behold, after them sprouted seven ears, thin and blighted by the east wind. And the thin ears swallowed up the seven plump and full ears. And Pharaoh awoke, and behold, it was a dream. So in the morning his spirit was troubled; and he sent and called for all the magicians of Egypt and all its wise men; and Pharaoh told them his dream, but there was none who could interpret it to Pharaoh" *(Genesis 41:1-8).*

CANDLEMAS FEB. 2

The name comes from the candles that are blessed, lighted, and distributed to worshipers on this date. The candles are then carried in a procession in church. Candlemas commemorates the visit of the Holy Family to the temple *(Luke 2:22).* On this same occasion, an elderly prophetess named Anna recognized Jesus as the Savior of the world.

> "And when the time came for their purification according to the law of Moses, they brought Him up to Jerusalem to present Him to the Lord."
>
> *(Luke 2:22)*

BIBLE VALENTINES

Valentines make us think of love and devotion to others, virtues we read about in the Bible.

"You shall love your neighbor as yourself."

(Leviticus 19:17-18)

"This I command you, to love one another."

(John 15:17)

And another from John, perhaps one of the best-known Biblical verses about love: "For God so loved the world that He gave His only Son, that whoever believes in Him should not perish but have eternal life."

(John 3:16)

"You shall love your neighbor as yourself."
LEVITICUS 19:17-18

VALENTINE'S DAY—FEBRUARY 14

People give each other valentines on this date as a symbol of love and affection. The valentines are usually heart-shaped, or have heart-like drawings, sweet verses, and promises of love. The preferred color of valentines is red.

Make a valentine heart cake or a decoupage as a valentine gift.

VALENTINE HEART CAKE

As you make the cake, think of giving it to someone to show your Christian love.

"It is better to give than to receive" *(Acts 20:35)*. This passage helps you to understand that no one is too small to show love by giving.

DIRECTIONS FOR MAKING A VALENTINE HEART CAKE

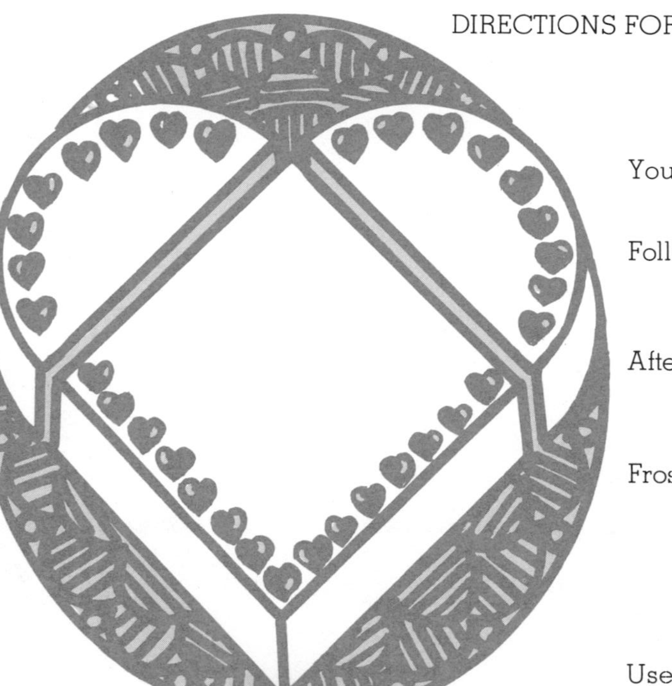

You will need one square pan, one round pan.

Follow the directions on a white cake mix package and pour batter into the tins. Bake according to directions.

After cake cools, cut round layer in half. Place each half at an angle to the square layer.

Frost with any white frosting mix. You can use red food coloring to give the frosting a pink or red color. Then decorate as you like. The cake looks pretty on a plate with a lace doily under it.

Use red candy hearts on the outer edges of the cake.

(John 3:16)

Make Valentines from construction paper and inscribe on them your favorite Scripture passage. (Begin with the ones cited here, but try to find others as well.)

A VALENTINE GIFT DIRECTIONS FOR DECOUPAGE

You will need pictures from magazines or some you make out of construction paper; a piece of scrap wood; sandpaper; and shellac.

Take a square piece of wood and sand the edges until smooth. Glue on pictures or your own decorations. Let dry thoroughly. Cover with one coat of shellac. Let dry and cover with a second coat of shellac. You can nail in a small picture hanger on the back if you wish.

Since Valentine's Day celebrates love, think about these Bible passages:

"But I say to you, Love your enemies and pray for those who persecute you."
(Matthew 5:44)

And, "If you love Me you will keep My commandments."
(John 14:15)

Talk about these Bible passages as you celebrate Valentine's Day.

NATURAL WONDERS OF THE WORLD

There are seven natural wonders of the world; one of them is listed below among three choices. If you do not know the correct choice, look it up in a world book or encyclopedia. The Bible speaks of other wonders:

The three choices are:

Everglades in Florida;
Carlsbad Caverns in New Mexico;
Mammoth Cave in Kentucky.

"And I will show wonders in the heaven above and signs on the earth beneath, blood, and fire, and vapor of smoke."
(Acts 2:19)

God's creation is full of wonders, as He reminded Job:

"Hear this, O Job; stop and consider the wondrous works of God. Do you know how God lays His command upon them, and causes the lightning of His cloud to shine? Do you know the balancings of the clouds, the wondrous works of Him who is perfect in knowledge?"
(Job 37:14-16)

(correct: Carlsbad Caverns)

Wallowitch

SHARING

We feel like sharing when we feel good about ourselves and others. Sometimes we speak of this "sharing feeling" as peace of mind.

> Jesus said: "I am leaving you with a gift—peace of mind and heart! And the peace I give isn't fragile like the peace the world gives. So don't be troubled or afraid. Remember what I told you—I am going away, but I will come back to you again. If you really love Me, you will be very happy for Me, for now I can go to the Father, who is greater than I am."
>
> *(John 14:27-28)*

When you are kept inside the house by bad weather or illness, why not use this time to get together with a few friends or family members and have a *sharing time*. Here are some things you can do together:

A) Write a poem and share it. Each person can do this. Maybe the first poem can be about sharing.
B) Paint a picture. If someone likes your painting, or if you like someone's, perhaps giving the picture away, or exchanging, would be desirable.
C) Sing songs—some hymns about sharing, or new songs you make up yourself. You might make up new words to go with a favorite tune.
D) Play the piano or another musical instrument for the enjoyment of others.
E) Read a suitable Bible passage.
F) Think about, and discuss, the Bible passage.
G) Make a snack to share with others.

ARE YOU A "BACKWARD" SPELLER?

Have everyone sit in a circle. Select a leader. The leader calls out a Biblical word such as God, Lord, heaven, Scripture, etc., to the first speller. The speller must spell the word backwards and give its meaning. If the word is spelled wrong the player is out. The last one in the circle is the winner and becomes the next leader.

MARCH

REBIRTH

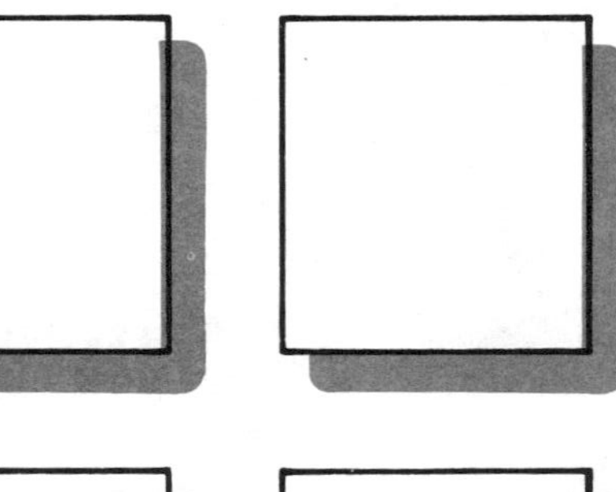

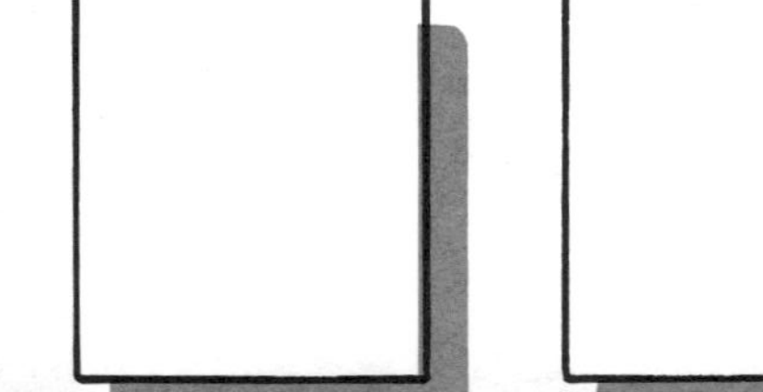
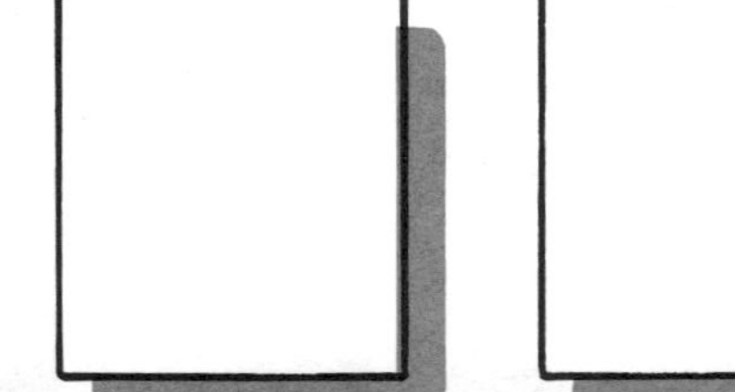

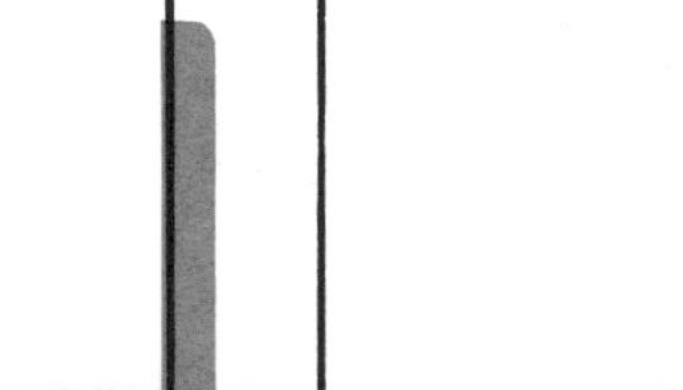
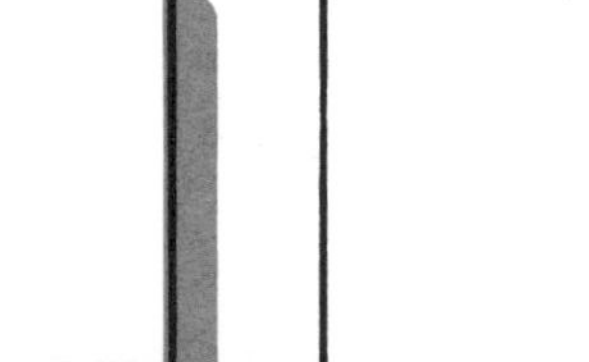

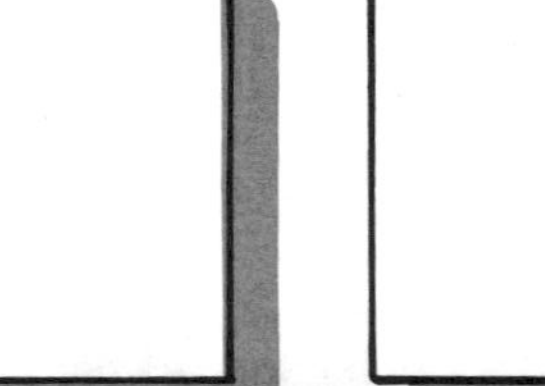

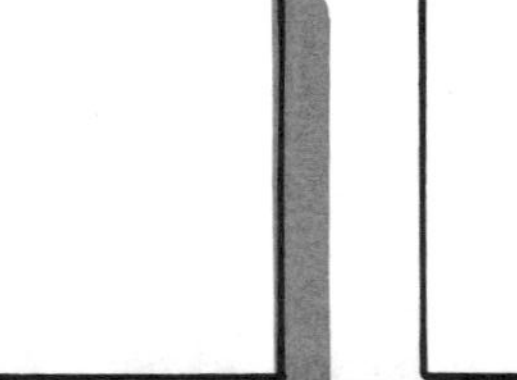

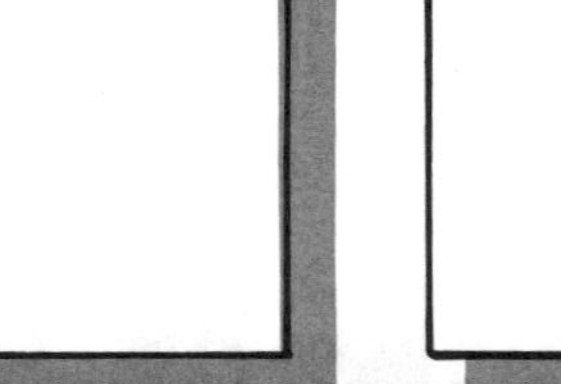
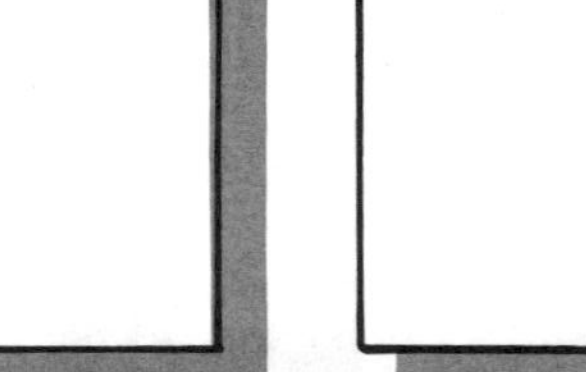
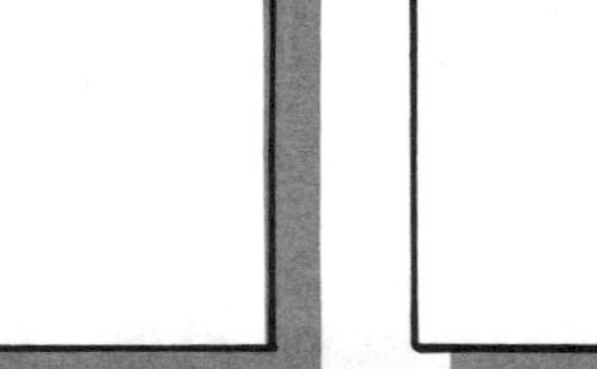
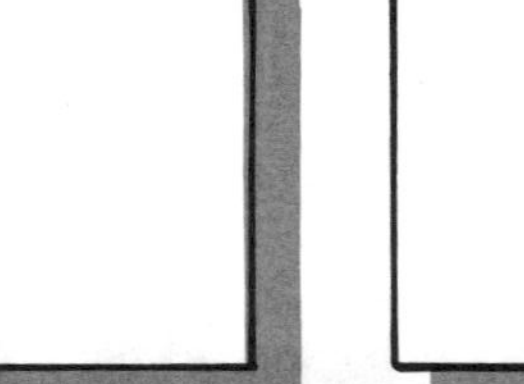

MARCH

GOD TALKS TO US

Spring is a time for rebirth, for resurrection, for life.

> "Jesus said to her, 'I am the Resurrection and the Life; he who believes in Me, though he die, yet shall he live; and whoever lives and believes in Me shall never die."
> *(John 11:25-27)*

> "He has risen from the dead, and behold, He is going before you to Galilee; there you will see Him."
> *(Matthew 27:6-7)*

> "If we have been united with Him in a death like His, we shall certainly be united with Him in a resurrection like His."
> *(Romans 6:5)*

Discuss these passages with your family and friends and try to understand the general meaning of "rebirth" or resurrection.

	1st WEEK	2nd WEEK	3rd WEEK	4th WEEK	5th WEEK
SUNDAY					
MONDAY					
TUESDAY					
WEDNESDAY					

BIRTHSTONE:

Bloodstone

FLOWER:

Jonquil

BIRTHDATES OF PRESIDENTS:

Andrew Jackson
Born: March 15, 1767

James Madison
Born: March 16, 1751

Grover Cleveland
Born: March 18, 1837

John Tyler
Born: March 29, 1790

THURSDAY

FRIDAY

SATURDAY

THINGS TO DO–

REBIRTH

SONG OF SPRING

Spring means rebirth, resurrection, the promise of new life.

> "For lo, the winter is past, the rain is over and gone; the flowers appear on the earth; the time of the singing of birds is come, and the voice of the turtledove is heard in our land."
> *(Song of Solomon 2:11-12)*

> "To everything there is a season, and a time to every purpose under the heaven: A time to be born, and a time to die; a time to plant, and a time to pluck up that which is planted."
> *(Ecclesiastes 3:1-2)*

PEOPLE AND ANIMALS IN BIBLE STORIES

THE GARDEN OF GETHSEMANE

Draw or construct the Garden of Gethsemane. If you draw it, show Jesus with three other men (Peter and the two sons of Zebedee). Make the garden green and full of flowers, with a desert in the distance. If you construct the garden, place it in a small sandbox, putting in trees, green grass, a stream. What kind of tree would you use? (Palm?)

> "Then Jesus went with them to a place called Gethsemane, and He said to His disciples, 'Sit here, while I go yonder and pray.' And taking with Him Peter and the two sons of Zebedee, He began to be sorrowful and troubled."
> *(Matthew 26:36-37)*

Listed below are several names of persons and animals mentioned in the Bible. Connect the ones that go together:

Daniel	Great fish
Eve	Lion
Jonah	Ram
Abraham	Snake
Wise Men	Camel

(You can find the answers in the following Bible verses):

Daniel	Daniel 6:16
Eve	Genesis 3:1
Jonah	Jonah 1:17
Abraham	Genesis 22:13
Wise Men	Matthew 2:1

CODED MESSAGE

Uncode this message. It is a prayer from the Bible. (Circle every fifth letter to get the message.)

IEYSOQEUOUURIWRETODFAFSJAJFIWT

ZGSBHMFIQEMVJDRBZCAWAGSBHMVJ

SOPYICAKDUQRHSYQTAFJOIPNZVNHDF

AHJFIREWGCKANVZHVBCTQEIPDNNLJG

SHHDNCAOURPLQETULITYSOGDBCWZ

CYEELFIQDGSUPBHAGWELPHVTBDYUHX

ARQYORHINHFKSABXNIMYQDRE.

After you have decoded the message, look up the following passage in the Bible, check your accuracy, and note the rest of the prayer. *(Matthew 6:9)*

THE TWELVE APOSTLES

Who were the twelve apostles? Try to name as many as you can before looking at the following list: ("He called His disciples; and chose from them twelve, whom He named apostles: *Simon,* whom he named *Peter,* and *Andrew* his brother, and *James* and *John,* and *Philip,* and *Bartholomew,* and *Matthew,* and *Thomas,* and *James* the son of Alphaeus, and *Simon* who was called the Zealot, and *Judas* the son of James, and *Judas Iscariot,* who became a traitor" *(Luke 6:13-16).*

Draw each apostle as you imagine he would look. Begin with a cylinder-shaped form; add face and beard, headdress, garment (you can make many different colored garments with bows or ropes); and write the name under each drawing.

You can vary their looks by coloring some beards light brown, some very dark or black, some reddish; you can also color the garments differently.

If you wish, make the apostles out of cardboard, using light-colored cloth for garments (old handkerchiefs might do). Pipe stems can be used for sashes. Or just look around your house and find other decorative materials.

SCRAMBLED VERSES

The verses as written do not make sense. Unscramble them and write them down on a piece of paper.

A) My messenger send, Behold, I face Thy before way Thy shall who prepare. *(Mark 1:2)*

B) worship God shall Lord the You your. *(Luke 4:8)*

C) anew born is one the he see cannot unless truly truly say I God kingdom of you to. *(John 3:3)*

(After you have tried to unscramble the words, look up the references in the Bible to see if you were correct, or to help you finish the passage.)

WORD MATHEMATICS

In each of the examples below there are parts of words plus symbols (or drawing) that make up a whole word. Some of these are from the Bible; write in the whole word.

1. [drawing] + le __________
   (The __________ is the word of God.)

2. [drawing] + ch __________

3. [drawing: GO] + d __________
   (__________ created the heavens and the earth.)

4. [drawing: MATH FINAL] + ament __________
   (The old/new __________ are two parts of the Bible.)

5. St + [drawing] __________

WALK-ALONG PAPER FINGER PUPPETS

Following the directions given below, you can make paper finger puppets of various Biblical characters. Recite the Bible story, using the finger puppet as the "speaker."

Here's how you make the finger puppets:

On heavy paper, draw any kind of person or animal (you may want to draw one or more of the apostles, for example). Do not draw legs on your puppet, but allow an extra 1½ inches at bottom of your drawing. Cut out two holes for your fingers in the 1½" allowed. Fold this 1½" back and put your fingers through the holes. Your fingers become the legs of the puppet.

Have the finger puppets "speak" some of the following passages from the Bible: "Repent, for the kingdom of heaven is at hand" *(Matthew 3:2)*. Or, "Prepare the way of the Lord, make His paths straight" (*Mark 1:3*).

6. + thew ______________
(______________ is the first book of the New Testament.)

7. Y + ______________
(My ______________ of redemption has come. *Isaiah 63:4)*

8.  + ian ______________
(You think to make me a ______________. *Acts 26:28)*

9. Wor +  ______________
(O come, let us ______________ and bow down. *Psalm 95:6)*

10.  + M ______________
(So they took branches of ______________ trees and went out to meet Him. *John 12:13*)

11. 

+ ah ______________
(They went into the ark with ______________. *Genesis 7:15)*

WONDERS OF THE ANCIENT WORLD

Some books have said there were *seven* wonders of the ancient world. Three choices are listed below; one of them is correct.

a) The Hanging Gardens of Babylon
b) The River Nile
c) The desert

"By the waters of Babylon, there we sat down and wept, when we remembered Zion. On the willows there we hung up our lyres" *(Psalm 134:1-2).*

(Correct: Hanging Gardens of Babylon)

"FEELY-BAG" (MEMORY GAME)

Instructions: One person who is not playing the game (maybe your mother or father) is to place 8—12 objects in a large paper bag. Each person playing the game looks into the bag for *just 30 seconds* to try to remember the contents.

When the bag is closed he/she must tell what was in the bag, or if possible list the articles on a piece of paper.

The one who remembers the most objects wins the game.

Children who do not remember all the items in the bag can place their hands in the bag, feel around, and try to discover the articles they had forgotten were there. This helps even the smallest player to "remember" better.

Articles for the bag: cross; a small Bible; a small tennis or other ball; some string; a small picture of Jesus; a hymn-book; a program or lesson from Sunday school or church; a leaf (or small branch) from a tree; a favorite storybook (small); a piece of large paper on which is written a favorite Bible verse; a picture of someone you love.

MAKE YOUR OWN BEAUTIFUL GARDEN

You have heard and read in the Bible the stories about the Garden of Eden and the Garden of Gethsemane. Although we cannot recreate these beautiful gardens now, you can make your own garden. This will help you to appreciate the beauty of spring, the way things grow, and the beauty of gardens.

You can make crystals in your own home with salt (which is a crystal) and watch them grow daily.

HERE'S WHAT YOU WILL NEED:

¼ cup of salt;
¼ cup of bluing;
¼ cup of ammonia;
4-6 charcoal briquettes;
aluminum pie or cake pan;
jar with a lid;
measuring cup;
food coloring.

HERE'S WHAT YOU DO:

1. Place the 4-6 charcoal briquettes in the aluminum pan.
2. Pour salt, bluing, and ammonia into a jar; mix together.
3. Sprinkle drops of food coloring on the briquettes.
4. Pour the salt/bluing/ammonia mixture evenly over the charcoal briquettes.
5. Set the pan in a warm place.
6. The crystals will start to grow in a short time; watch for the growth.
7. Mix the same solution of salt, bluing, and ammonia in jar again.
8. Add this new solution to your garden every few days to keep it growing.

APRIL

JESUS
CHRIST THE SAVIOR

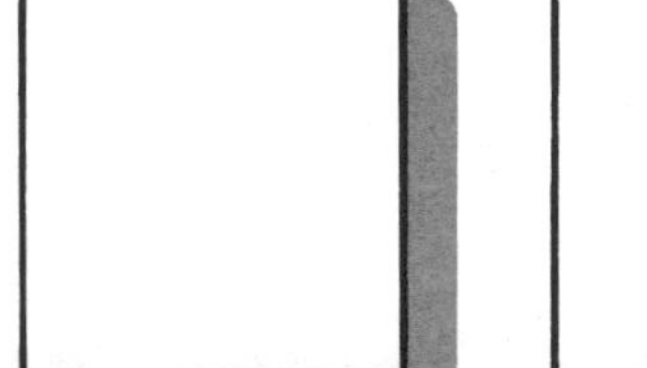
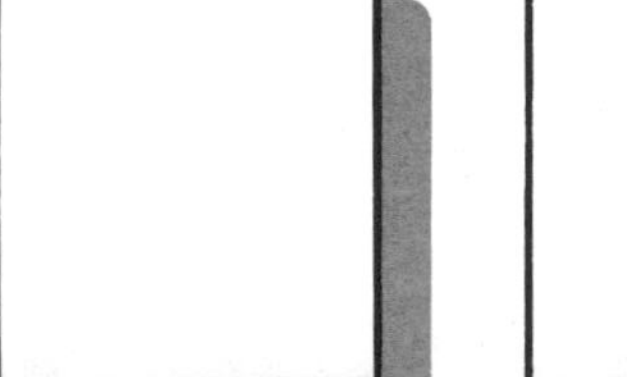
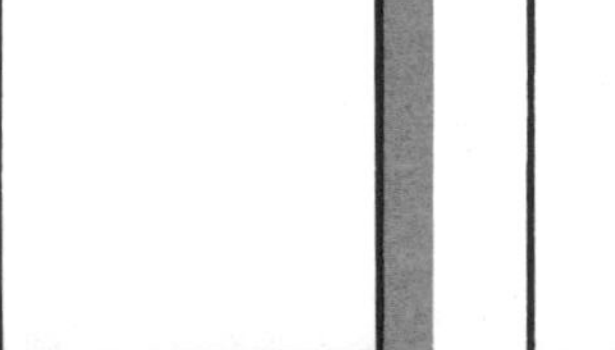
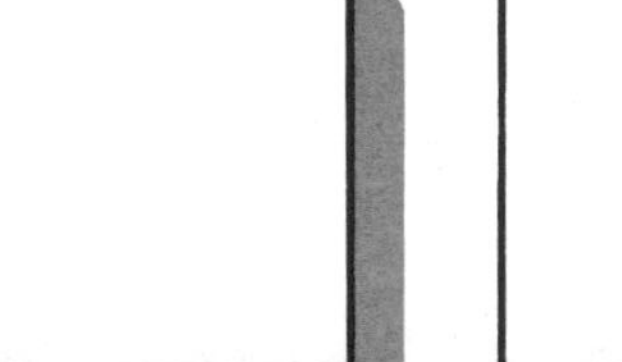
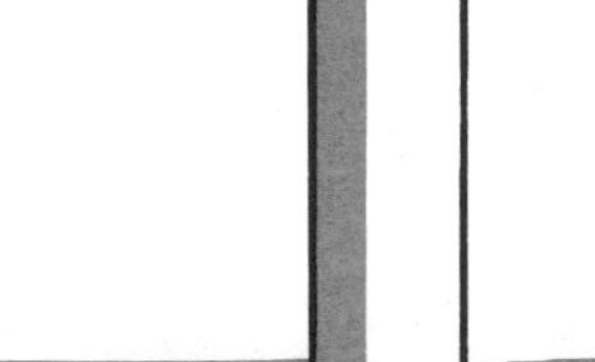
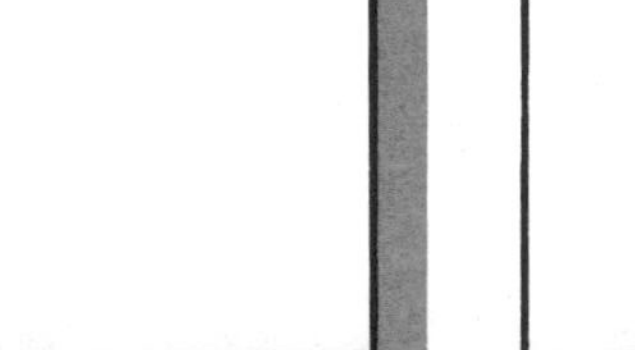
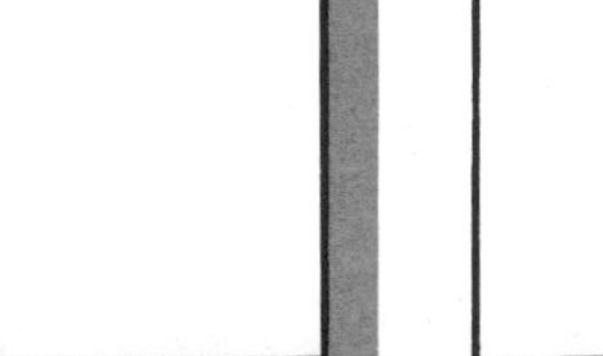
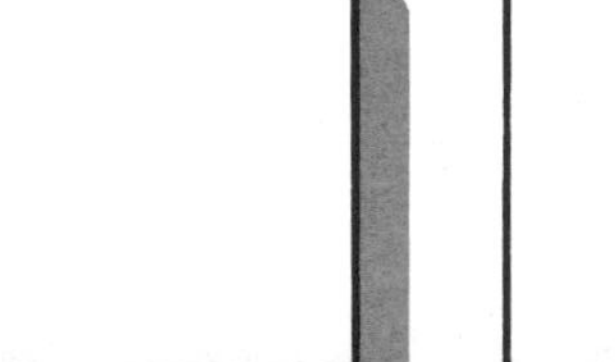
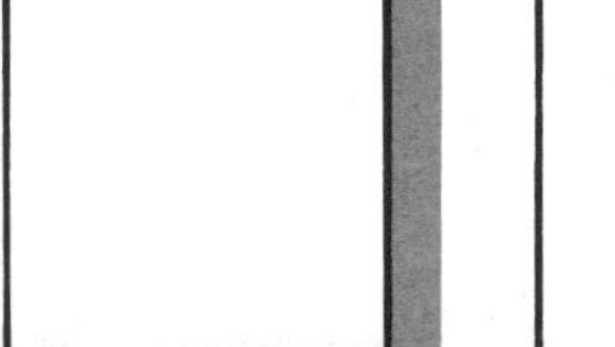

APRIL

BIRTHSTONE:

Diamond

The symbol of courage. "Be strong, and let your heart take courage, all you who wait for the Lord" *(Psalm 31:24).*

FLOWER:

Sweet Pea, Daisy

Did you know that the petals of a daisy close at night? That's where the name came from. It was once known as "day's eye" because it is open only during the day.

BIRTHDATES OF PRESIDENTS/ FAMOUS PEOPLE:

Thomas Jefferson
Born: April 13, 1743

James Buchanan
Born: April 23, 1791

	1st WEEK	2nd WEEK	3rd WEEK	4th WEEK	5th WEEK
SUNDAY					
MONDAY					
TUESDAY					
WEDNESDAY					

Ulysses S. Grant
Born: April 27, 1822

Hans Christian Anderson
(Writer of children's stories)
Born: April 2, 1805

Washington Irving
(Early American writer)
Born: April 3, 1783

Leonardo da Vinci
(Painter of religious themes)
Born: April 10, 1452

April is an important month for Christian festivals. Easter most often falls in April, with other special days such as Maundy Thursday and Good Friday also occurring near the same time.

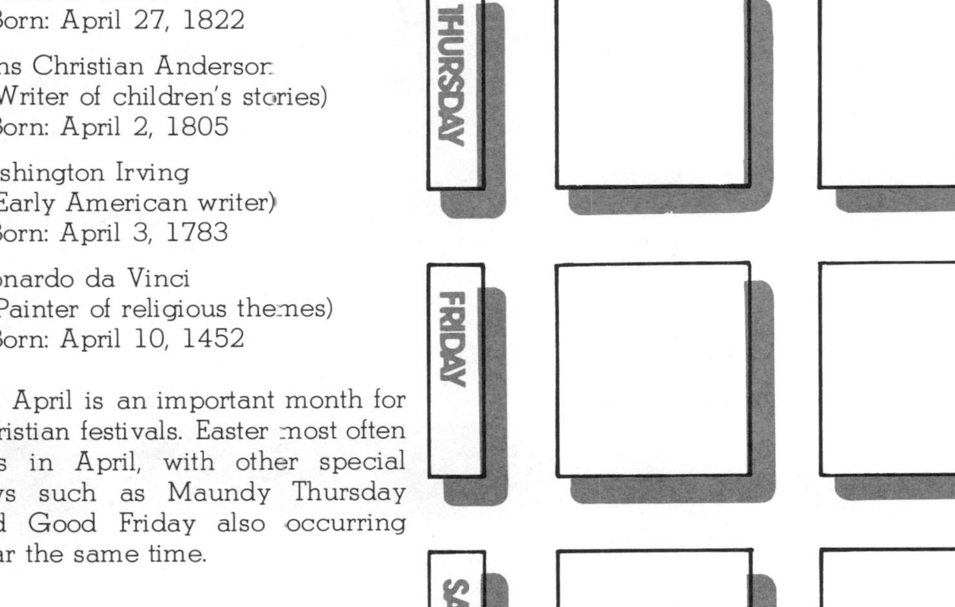

THINGS TO DO–

JESUS CHRIST THE SAVIOR

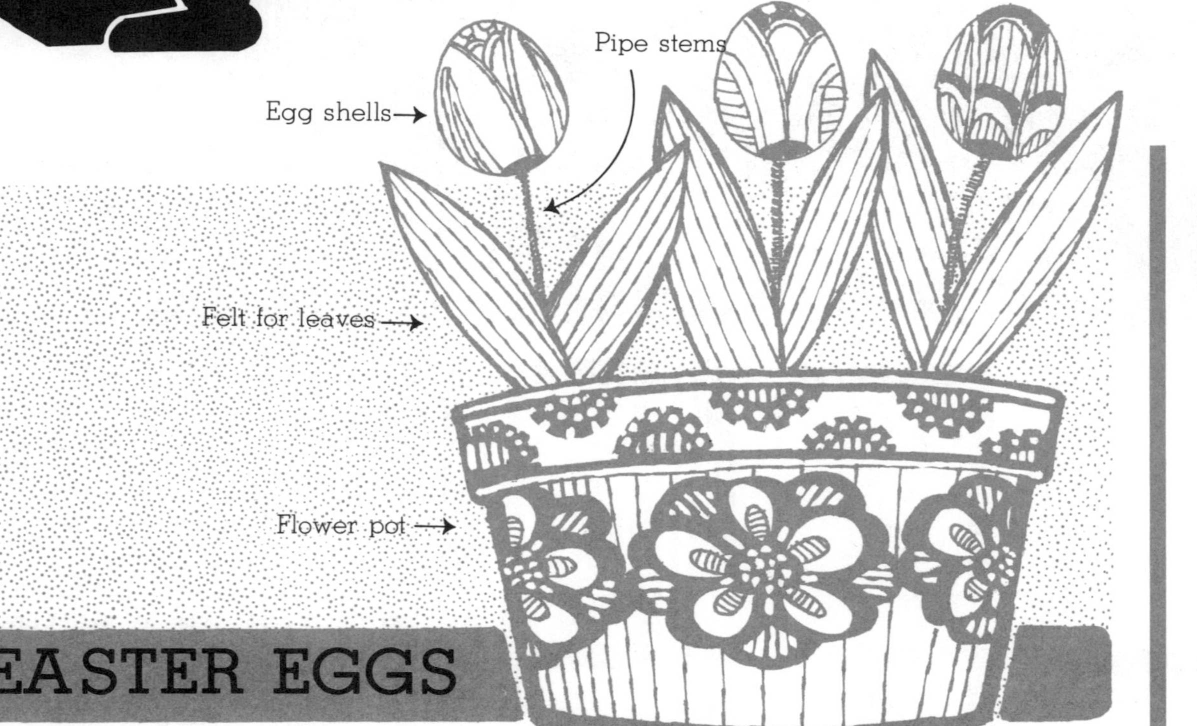

EASTER EGGS

Make a tulip (or other flower) garden with eggs, pipe cleaner, felt, and a magic marker.

Blow out the inside of several eggs. Handle gently so they don't break. Put a pin into this same small hole (from which you get out the inside of the egg), and twist it around to make the hole a bit larger. Then put a pipe cleaner into the same hole. Pushing the other end of the pipe cleaner into some soil in a small flower pot.

Now you have the egg shell stuck on the pipe cleaner and the other end inserted into soil. Now color the egg shell with a magic marker (use lots of colors!) to decorate it.

Next, cut out some leaf shapes from the felt. Glue the felt leaf shapes onto the pipe cleaner just below the egg shell, so that now you have "leaves" on the stem (or pipe cleaner).

Now you have a lovely little flower garden to brighten someone's room.

APRIL MESSAGE

"Now after the sabbath, toward the dawn of the first day of the week, Mary Magdalene and the other Mary went to see the sepulchre. And behold, there was a great earthquake; for an angel of the Lord descended from heaven and came and rolled back the stone, and sat upon it. His appearance was like lightning, and his raiment white as snow. And for fear of him the guards trembled and became like dead men. But the angel said to the women, 'Do not be afraid; for I know that you seek Jesus who was crucified. He is not here; for He has risen, as He said. Come, see the place where He lay" *(Matthew 28:1-6).*

MAKE YOUR OWN CHURCH CHIMES

PLANT STARTERS AND HELPERS

The weather is getting warmer; it may be warm enough in most areas to begin seedlings and plants indoors, or even outdoors. Some ideas are:

1. Cut off the top of a pineapple and place fruit end down in a pan of shallow water. Let it root; then plant in soil for a Pineapple Palm.

2. Take a sweet potato and stick toothpicks around it (or you might prefer to use an avocado seed instead). Place the sweet potato (or avocado seed) over the top of a glass of water, with the toothpicks holding it. Let it root; plant it in soil and watch a small tree grow.

← Sweet Potato (or avocado seed)

Toothpicks

← Glass of water (3/4 full)

(Note: Plants like to be clean, so wipe plant leaves with a 1-to-1 mixture of water and milk, for a cleansing and nourishing bath.)

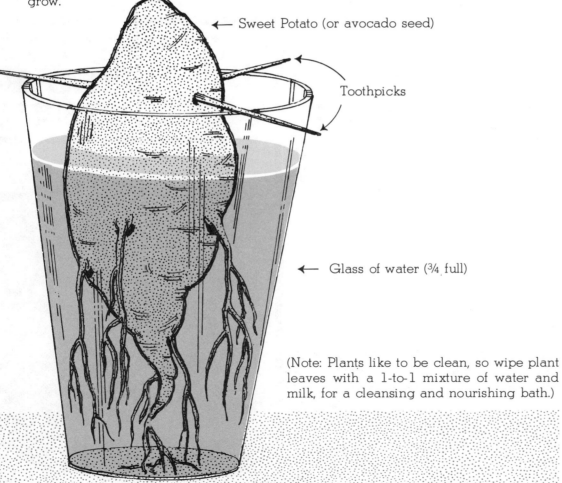

Make a musical scale to play favorite church songs or hymns. All you need are eight classes (about the same size), water, and a spoon.

Fill one glass nearly full with water. Line up the other 7 glasses so you fill them, step-wise, with less and less water, until the last glass has barely any water in it.

Tap the glasses lightly with a spoon and note the sound (pitch). As the amount of water gets less and less in successive glasses, the sound (pitch) will get higher. You can add or subtract water in any glass to control the sound.

Now begin your music—chimes (like church chimes), hymns, or songs you make up yourself.

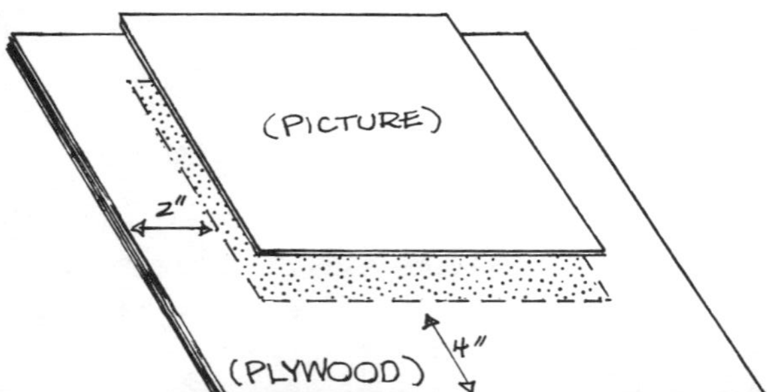

EASTER CROSS CAKE RECIPE

Do you know any people in nursing homes or hospitals, or any children confined at home because of illness, who might enjoy this delightful and delicious cake around Easter time? If you were ill or in the hospital, you might be very pleased to receive such a thoughtful gift. Recall the Bible passage:

"So whatever you wish that men would do to you, do so to them; for this is the Law and the prophets."

(Matthew 7:12)

Follow the directions on any cake mix package, pouring the batter into two oblong cake pans. Bake according to directions. Cool.

Take one of the oblong (or rectangular) cake layers and cut it in thirds.

	cut	

Lay the other oblong cake layer on a tray and place each of the pieces on *opposite* sides of the oblong cake, to make a cross.

You can move the cut halves up higher or down lower to get the shape you like best. Next, frost and decorate.

You might decorate your cake with lavender, yellow, and pink flowers. Now you have an Easter cross cake! Think carefully about what you will do with it.

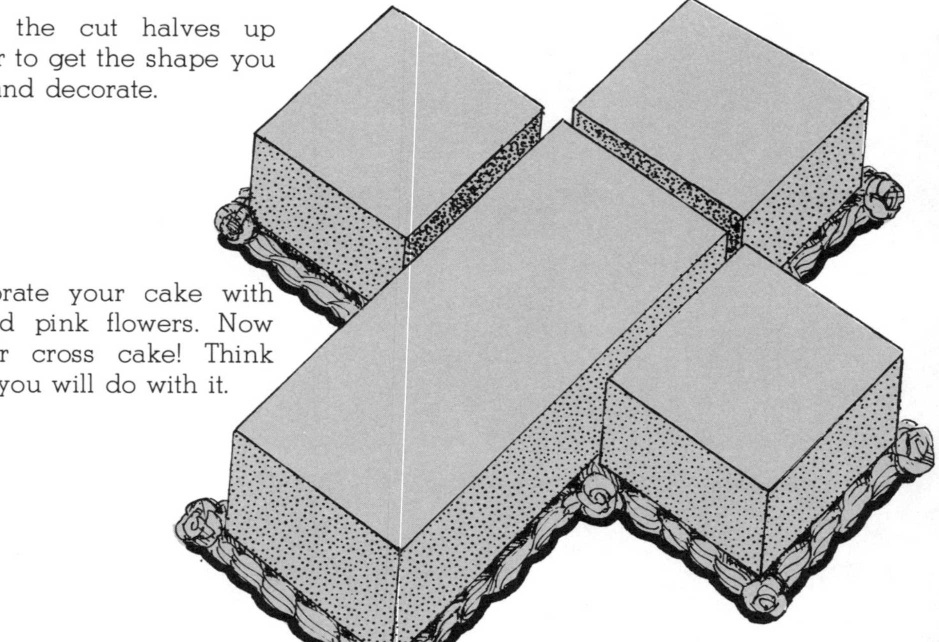

IMAGE OF CHRIST (DECOUPAGE)

Definition of decoupage: the technique of decorating a surface with paper cutouts.

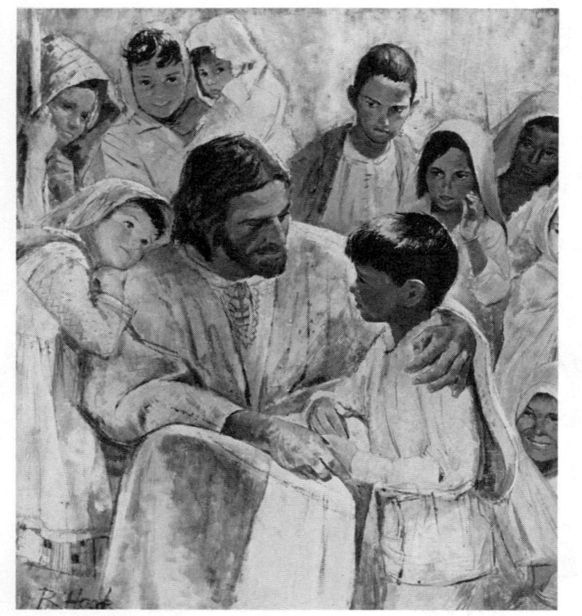

First get a picture of Christ, as large or small as you can find and use. A picture about 8" x 11" would be practical.

Next, glue the picture to a larger square of light plywood or heavy cardboard, so that you have a border of 2" to 4" all the way around.

Decorate the border (unless you prefer to leave it white or just one color) with colorful designs, such as crosses, nature scenes, or something of your own choosing.

Mount the final image on a dresser or desk, or hang on the wall. (To hang the image, you will need a small nail hole in the top.) Give this to your mother or father (or both) for Easter.

> "Then children were brought to Him that He might lay His hands on them and pray" *(Matthew 19:13)*

JESUS CHRIST THE SAVIOR

The name "Jesus" means Savior.

> "You shall call His name Jesus, for He will save His people from their sins." *(Matthew 1:21b)*

> "The Son of Man [Jesus] came to seek and to save the lost." *(Luke 19:10)*

> "God so loved the world that He gave His only Son, that whoever believes in Him should not perish but have eternal life." *(John 3:16)*

APRIL PUZZLE

Begin at the *flower* on the umbrella and then read the first letter on the right, then every *second* letter, left to right, through all the letters on the umbrella. What is the message? (Hint: "April showers . . .")

As you work out this puzzle, think of the following Bible verse:

> "Thou makest springs gush forth in the valleys; they flow between hills, they give drink to every beast of the field . . . by them the birds of the air have their habitation; they sing among the branches." *(Psalm 104:10-12)*

EASTER ANIMAL DOT-TO-DOT

Guess what animal this is. Fill in the face and give it to a child who might like an Easter present. You might glue shreds of cotton to this animal body to make it look even more real.

As you complete this drawing, think of the following Bible verse:

"The next day he saw Jesus coming toward him, and said,
'Behold, the Lamb of God, who takes away the sin of the world.'"

(John 1:29)

MAY

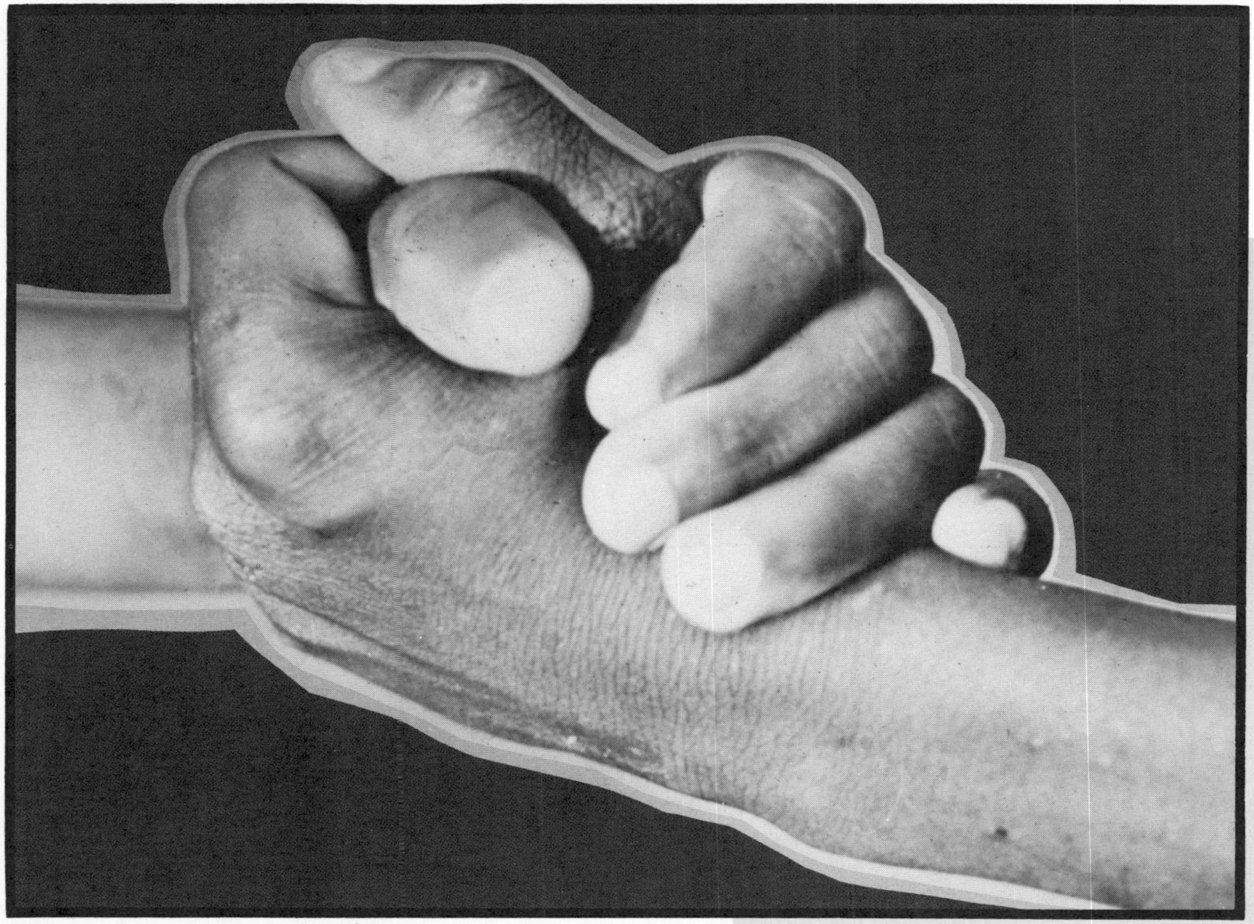

FRIENDSHIPS

MAY

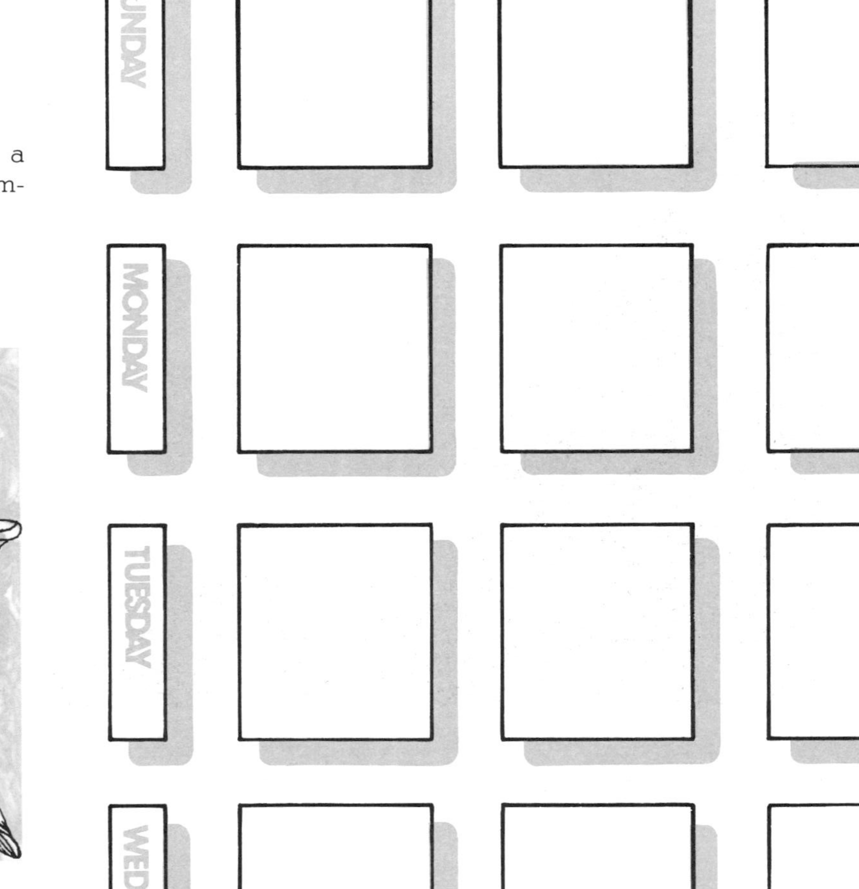

BIRTHSTONE:

Emerald

A highly valued gem with a clear, deep green color, symbolizing growth and spring.

FLOWER:

Lily of the Valley

This white, bell-like flower symbolizes purity and carries an attractive fragrance.

BIRTHDATES OF PRESIDENTS/ FAMOUS PEOPLE:

Harry S. Truman
Born: May 8, 1884

John F. Kennedy
Born: May 29, 1917

James J. Audubon
(Great naturalist and bird lover)
Born: May 4, 1780

Christopher Columbus
(Explorer, discoverer of America)
Born: May 5, 1435

Robert Browning
(English poet and writer)
Born: May 7, 1812

Florence Nightingale
(Humanist and hospital reformer)
Born: May 10, 1820

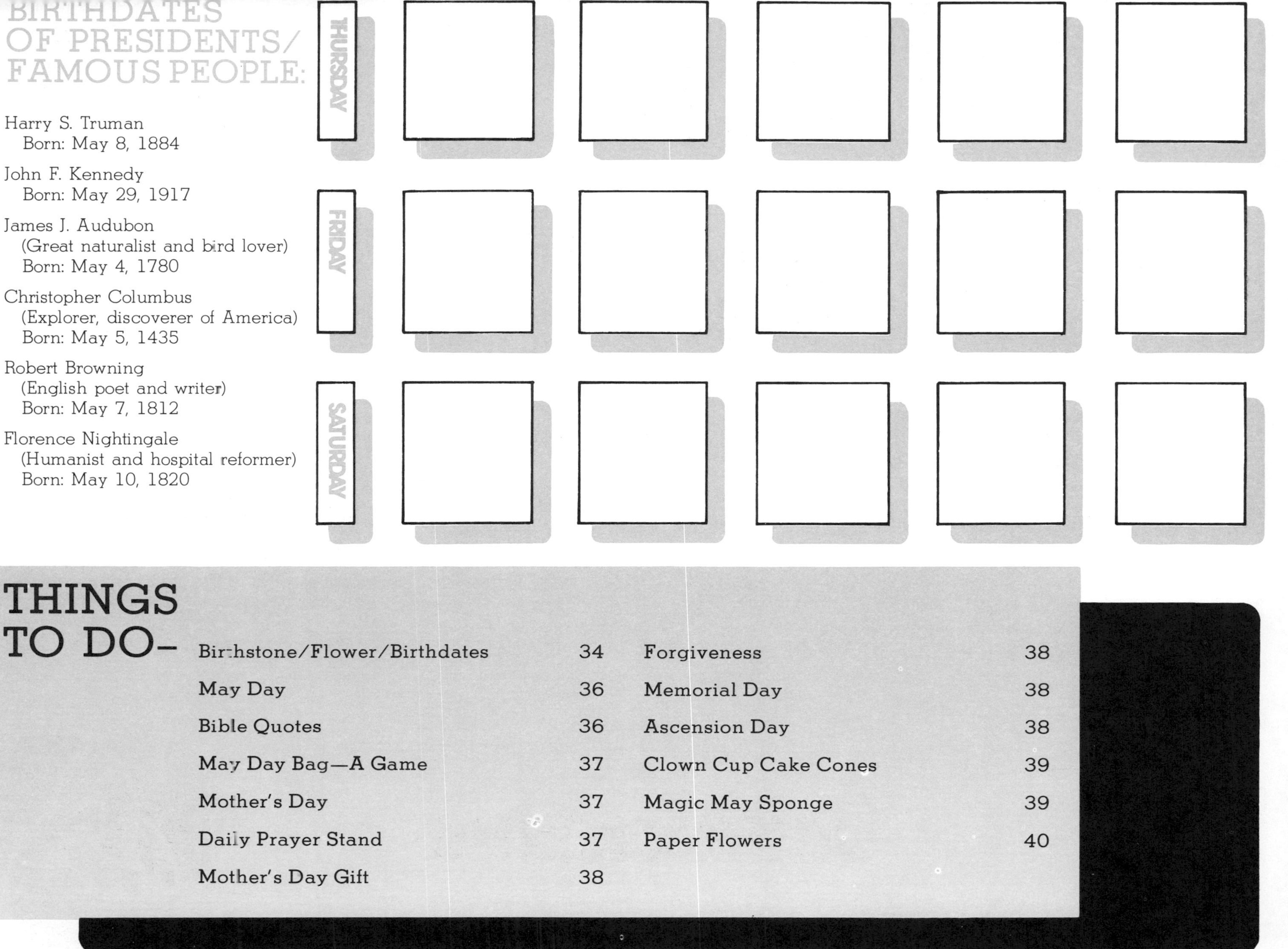

THINGS TO DO–

FRIENDSHIPS

MAY DAY

MAY 1 IS MAY DAY

It was originally a spring festival with religious significance observed in ancient Rome, with great emphasis on nature and on flowers.

May Day celebrates the return of life, the passing of winter, with new hopes for rich harvests. It is a day of rejoicing and singing which began many, many years ago and is still observed in the United States.

The color, beauty, and bountifulness of May help one to feel loving, kind, and friendly toward others.

The Bible says:

"A friend loves at all times."
(Proverbs 17:17)

Being a friend of other people is important, but being a friend of God is even better: "Abraham . . . was called the friend of God."
(James 2:22-23)

BIBLE QUOTES FOR THE HOME

Pick several of your favorite quotes from the Bible and type (or write, or print) them on small cardboard pieces (5" x 8", or 8" x 10", or any size you want).

Punch a hole in the top of the cardboard, or attach a string to the back, so that you can place the quotes on a dresser or desk, or hang from the wall.

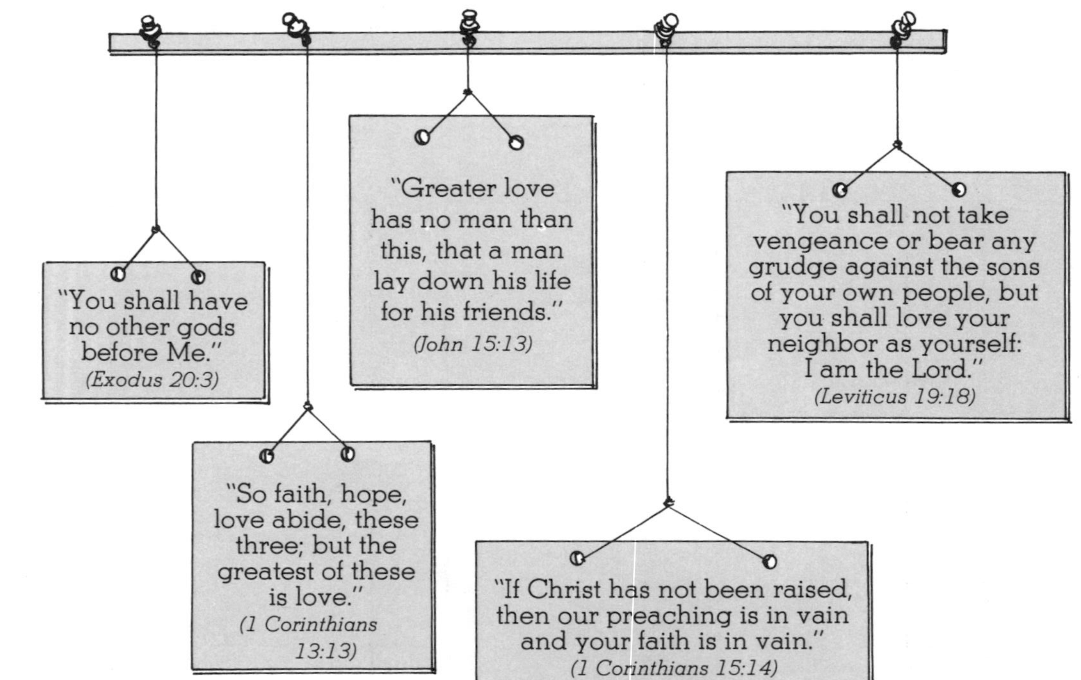

"You shall have no other gods before Me."
(Exodus 20:3)
"So faith, hope, love abide, these three; but the greatest of these is love."
(1 Corinthians 13:13)
"Greater love has no man than this, that a man lay down his life for his friends."
(John 15:13)
"If Christ has not been raised, then our preaching is in vain and your faith is in vain."
(1 Corinthians 15:14)
"You shall not take vengeance or bear any grudge against the sons of your own people, but you shall love your neighbor as yourself: I am the Lord."
(Leviticus 19:18)

MAY DAY BAG-A GAME

Fill a large paper bag with sweets, small toys, and other small things; tie a piece of ribbon or string around the top of the bag.

Then suspend the bag from a door frame with a string.

Blindfold several children in succession, one at a time. Give each one, in turn, a stick with which they must try to hit the bag. Each child is allowed one, two, or three trials. When a hole is made in the bag and the contents scattered on the floor, the children scramble for them.

This little game can be played at birthday parties, and on rainy days when you're inside.

MOTHER'S DAY

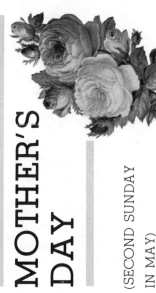

(SECOND SUNDAY IN MAY)

Although our present celebration of Mother's Day is fairly new (beginning with Pres. Woodrow Wilson's proclamation in 1914), God commands, "Honor your father and mother, that your days may be long in the land which the Lord your God gives you" *(Exodus 20:12)*. "A wise son makes a glad father, but a foolish son is a sorrow to his mother" *(Proverbs 10:1)*

DAILY PRAYER STAND

Make a cardboard stand like this ____________ and on the slanting part put a short prayer.

Make several such stands; or, after selecting several prayers, type or write (or print) them on sheets of paper. Then put a different prayer on the stand whenever you like. You might have one for each day of the week, or one for each Sunday in the month.

Here are some prayers you might use:

"Hear my prayer, O Lord, and give ear to my cry."

(Psalm 39:12)

"O Thou who hearest prayer! To Thee shall all flesh come on account of sins."

(Psalm 65:2)

"I will be glad and rejoice in Thee: I will sing praise to Thy name, O Thou most High."

(Psalm 9:2)

"O Lord our Lord, how excellent is Thy name in all the earth! who hast set Thy glory above the heavens."

(Psalm 8:1)

DIRECTIONS:

Get a discarded cardboard box from a drug or grocery store.

Cut a piece of cardboard so that it is wider at one end than at the other.

Then draw broken lines as in the diagram, starting the lines at the shorter end of the cardboard.

Fold the cardboard along the dotted lines, and then turn under this fold, which acts as a slanting base for the prayer stand. From a side view, the stand will look like this:

12″—13″

10″

12″—15″

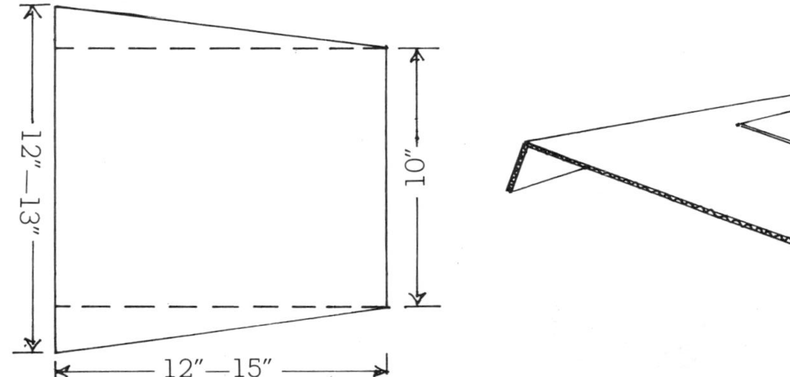

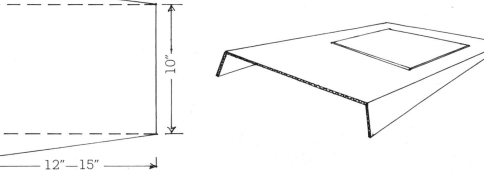

Then place a typed or written prayer on this stand. You could take it to Sunday school and use it yourself or let your teacher or some of the children use it.

MOTHER'S DAY GIFT

Collect an assortment of colorful fabric scraps (from old clothes and towels). Cut them carefully into different-sized rectangles and squares. Glue them one by one onto the outside of a small flowerpot. (You might find that the results are prettier if you overlap the pieces just a little.)

Now you have a lovely planter just waiting for a plant.

Your mother will like it too!

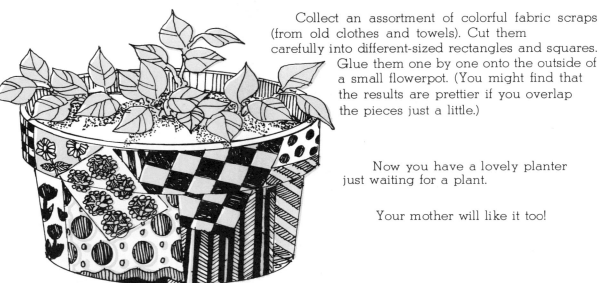

FORGIVENESS

The Bible tells us about God's forgiveness:

"If Thou, O Lord, shouldst mark iniquities, Lord, who could stand? But there is forgiveness with Thee, that Thou mayest be feared."

(Psalm 130:3-4)

We must repent and ask the Lord's forgiveness for our wrongdoing:

"And Peter said to them, 'Repent, and be baptized every one of you in the name of Jesus Christ for the forgiveness of your sins.'"

(Acts 2:28)

Often we fail to forgive our friends if they wrong us in some way.

Ask God to help you forgive others for their acts toward you. Ask forgiveness from your parents, friends, brothers, or sisters for your offenses against them.

"And forgive us our sins; for we also forgive everyone that is indebted to us."

(Luke 11:4)

"Judge not, and ye shall not be judged: condemn not, and ye shall not be condemned: forgive, and ye shall be forgiven."

(Luke 6:37)

MEMORIAL DAY

(MAY 30)

All the dead are remembered on this day. We honor our loved ones—family, friends, national heroes, etc.—with ceremonies, religious observances, prayers, and flowers or wreaths placed on their graves.

ASCENSION DAY

(40 DAYS AFTER EASTER)

This day celebrates Christ's ascent into heaven after rising from the dead. (See *Acts 1:6-11*).

"And He led them out as far as to Bethany, and He lifted up His hands, and blessed them. And it came to pass, while He blessed them, He was parted from them and carried up into heaven. And they worshiped Him and returned to Jerusalem with great joy."

(Luke 24:50-52).

CLOWN CUP CAKE CONES

For the cup cake cone, you will need:

ice cream cones with a flat bottom; cake mix; frosting mix; decorations (colored candies, thin licorice, large gumdrops). Make cake mix according to directions. Fill the cone one-half full; bake at 400 degrees F. 15—18 minutes; then let cool. Frost the top of the cake; decorate to look like a clown.

Use a gumdrop for the hat and thin licorice for hair. (Just stick it in the frosting.)

This cone is a great idea for a church bazaar, a gift to a sick friend, or a May Day prize.

MAGIC MAY SPONGE

Sponges *can* grow plants! Don't believe it? Try it!

Start with a fluffy sponge, the kind you buy for car washing. Sow seeds in the open pores of the sponge. Mustard seeds and watercress seeds (both edible) and birdseed will grow quickly, so they are good for the project.

After the seeds are in place, set the sponge in a shallow dish of water and let it "drink" its fill. Remove the sponge from the dish and tie it to a curtain rod in a sunny window, using a fishline or strong string for support.

Water the sponge *daily* by holding a dish of water up underneath the sponge, allowing it to get moist (but not too soggy or drippy).

The seeds will grow—just wait, watch, and see!

PAPER FLOWERS

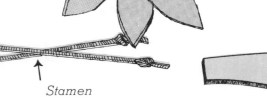

Wire

(Lily)

Petals

Stamen

Satin sheen ribbon, left over from your gift wrapping, can be made into beautiful flowers. You may use silk fabrics, tissue paper, or crepe paper, but ribbon will have more body.

Use 1" wide white ribbon. Cut three strips about 4" long. Point the ends for the lily of the valley. Overlap at the center to make six petals. Take a narrow strip of ribbon, and holding the petals at the center, tie petals together with a double knot. Curl tips under.

For stamens in the center, use two narrow yellow ribbons, tying knots at the ends of each, and tie at center to the center of the white petals. Add green speared leaves.

For the carnation, use pink, blue, and white ribbons, five or six strips. Use pinking shears on all the ends. Tie at center. Do not add stamens, but you may add a few dark spots at center with a felt tip. A long thin green ribbon may be added for the leaves. Curl the ends. Add a long thin wire for the stems.

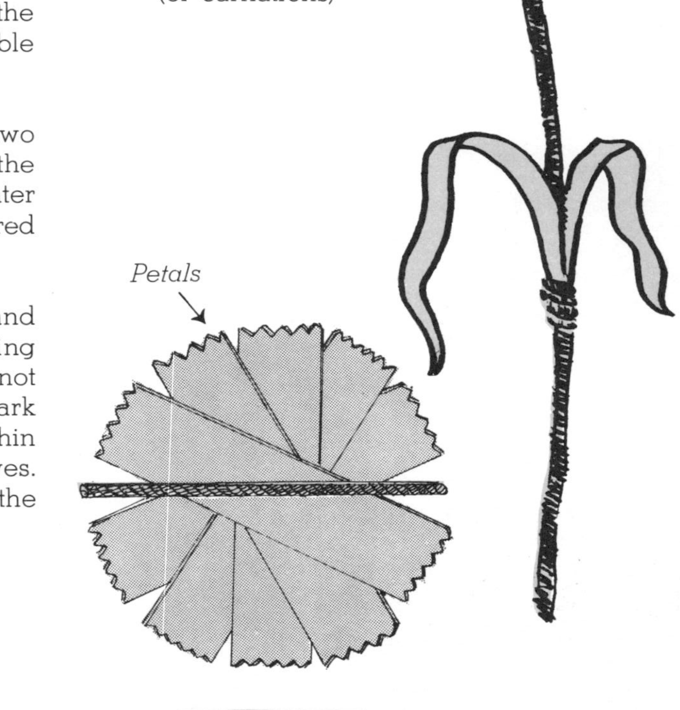

(or carnations)

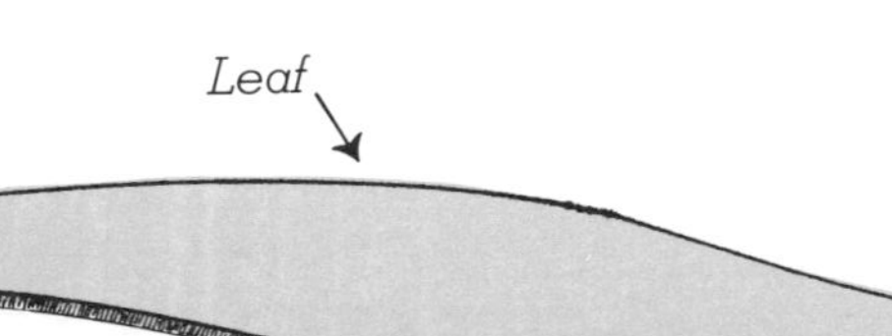

JUNE

ANIMALS IN THE BIBLE

JUNE

	1st WEEK	2nd WEEK	3rd WEEK	4th WEEK	5th WEEK
SUNDAY					
MONDAY					
TUESDAY					
WEDNESDAY					

BIRTHSTONE:

Pearl

FLOWER:

Rose

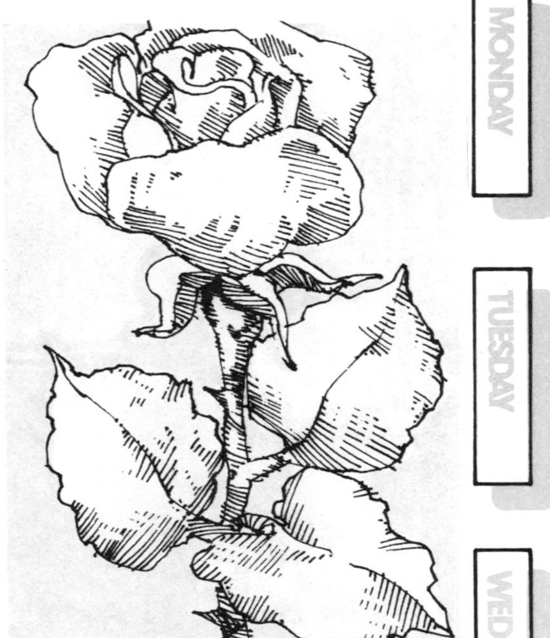

"The rose that lives its little hour is prized beyond the sculptured flower." (William Jennings Bryant)

BIRTHDATES OF PRESIDENTS/ FAMOUS PEOPLE:

Would you believe it? No American presidents were born during the month of June!

Robert Louis Stevenson
(Writer of children's stories and poetry)
Born: June 5, 1850

Helen Keller
(Blind, deaf woman who overcame great handicaps)
Born: June 10, 1880

Harriet Beecher Stowe
(American novelist)
Born: June 14, 1811

"And what is so rare as a day in June?"
("June Poem," James Russell Lowell)

THURSDAY

FRIDAY

SATURDAY

THINGS TO DO–

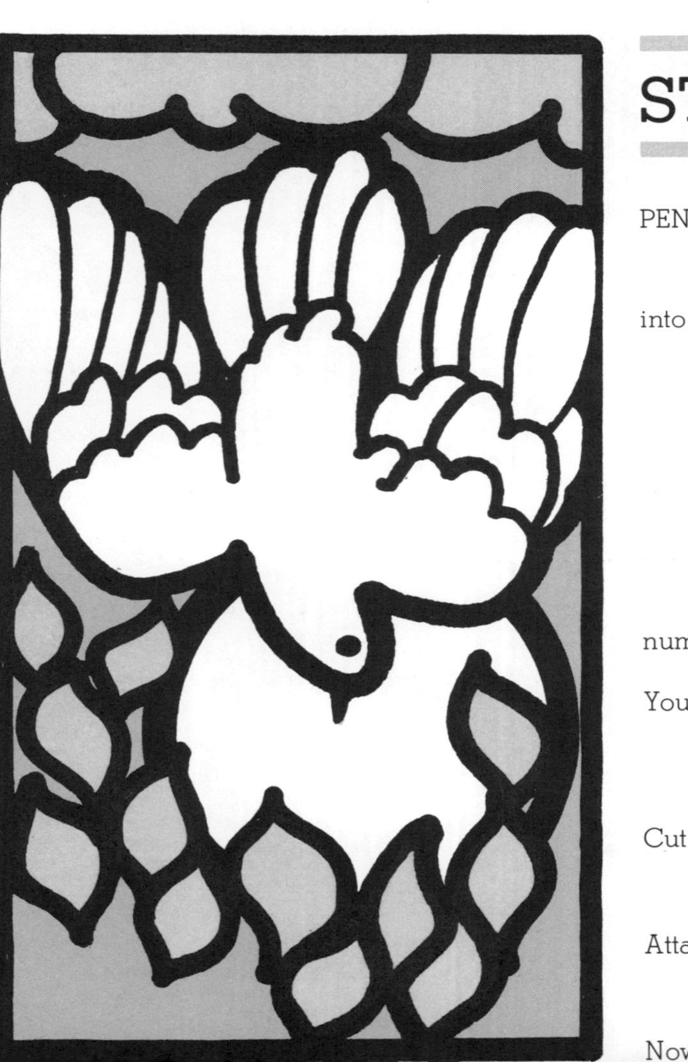

STAINED GLASS WINDOW

PENTECOST (OR WHITSUNDAY)

This day is celebrated 50 days after Easter, and 10 days after the ascension of Jesus Christ into heaven. Pentecost commemorates the descent of the Holy Spirit to the Christian church.

> "And there appeared to them tongues as of fire, distributed and resting on each one of them. And they were all filled with the Holy Spirit and began to speak in other tongues, as the Spirit gave them utterance."
>
> *(Acts 2:2-4)*

See Acts 1 and 2 for the full story of Pentecost.

Pentecost, sometimes called Whitsunday, comes seven weeks after Easter. Include this number in your stained glass window. Put "tongues of fire" in your stained glass window too.

You will need—

Colored cellophane (several different colors);
Narrow, black electrician's tape (small roll).

Cut designs from the cellophane.

(Try copying a simple church window, or make up your own picture from a Bible story.)

Attach the pieces to a window with the black tape.

(The black tape should be cut in thin strips to outline the cellophane figures.)

Now you have a stained glass window of your own!

FATHER'S DAY GIFT

The purpose of this day is to "honor and dignify fatherhood."

Find a favorite poem on "thanking" or on "love," or make up one of your own. Print the poem on a sheet of pretty paper (white poster paper might be good), and decorate it with flowers made with colored crayons. You may either frame it or decoupage it onto a board. Now you have a lovely gift that will remind your father how much you love him.

FATHER'S DAY CARD

Cut out a postcard-size piece from white or colored poster paper, about 5" x 8".

Draw and color on this card a copy of a picture you especially like from a Sunday school book or leaflet; or paste the picture on the card. Use only one side of the card.

Somewhere at the top of the picture you may want to write "To Dad, on Father's Day."

On the blank side of the card, draw a line down the middle to make it look like a regular postcard. On the right side, write out your father's name and home address: Mr. Ted Brown, 1234—56th St., Anytown, Anystate. On the left side, write, "My Dear Father," and then a note telling your father that you love and appreciate him. End it, "with love, from ________" and sign your name.

Draw Scene on Card

Original "Postcard"

My Dear Father,

With Love,
from your child
(signed)

Mr. Ted Brown
1234 . 56th St.
Anytown, Anystate
12345

Address to Father

FATHER'S DAY MESSAGE

(FATHER'S DAY—
THIRD SUNDAY IN JUNE)

God commands,

"Honor your father and your mother."
(Exodus 20:12)

And gives wise advice to fathers:

"Discipline your son while there is hope."
(Proverbs 19:18)

And a warning to children:

"If one curses his father or his mother, his lamp will be put out in utter darkness."
(Proverbs 20:20)

(The book of Proverbs has many worthwhile and thoughtful messages to fathers and children; you might want to look further into these.)

"My son, keep my words, and lay up my commandments with thee. Keep my commandments and live; and my law as the apple of thine eye."
(Proverbs 7:1-2).

FAMILY PICTURE ALBUM

This will be lots of fun!

Get some old pictures of your mother, father, grandparents, aunts, or uncles, and some more recent ones of the same people.

With a small amount of glue, fix each picture onto a page of paper. (Use white paper, or colored paper if you think a particular color fits a given person—for example, a reddish sheet of paper for your red-headed cousin Jane. Put only one picture on each page.

Put the earliest (or youngest) picture of a given person (mother, father, etc.) on the first page. Then on later pages put more recent (or later) pictures of the same person.

Do this for each person for whom you have one or more pictures.

You might want to write a caption for each person's picture:

"Mother in pigtails, age 8"
"Father in football uniform, age 15"
"Baby Cousin Joel getting a bath, age 1 year"
Etc.

What a laugh you and all the family members will have! They'll say, "Oh, no, did I look like that?" Or, "I thought I got rid of that horrible picture years ago!"

MAKE YOUR OWN ANIMAL COLORING BOOK

Get pictures of several animals you know and like—dogs, cats, elephants, bears, giraffes, etc.—and trace each one (or draw freely, if you can) on a separate sheet of paper.

Make as many animal drawings in outline form as you want.

Make a front cover sheet that says, "My Favorite Animals" or a similar title; and a back cover. You may want to put your name on the bottom of the front cover of your Animal Coloring Book.

Put small holes in the sides of each page, including the covers (or place the holes at the top, if you prefer), and tie the pages together with a piece of colored string or yarn.

You may want to keep this book and add to it as you discover or learn about more animals; or you may want to give the book to a brother, sister, or friend.

After the book is finished, you, or the person you give it to, can begin to color it. Be sure you have the right colors for the animals.

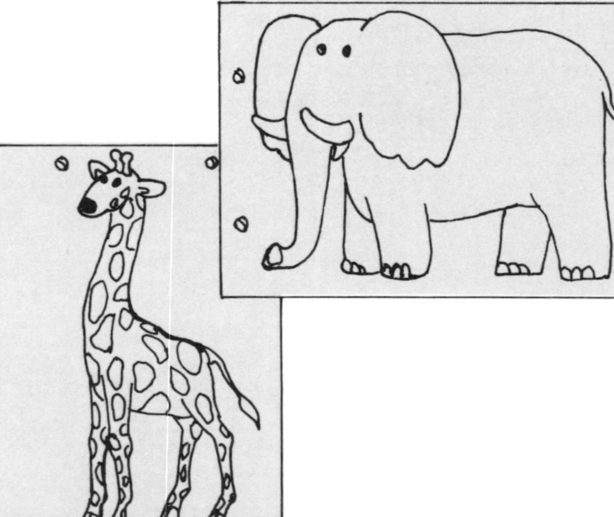

ANIMAL THEME

Animals are important because they are part of God's creation. The Book of Genesis tells the story of Noah, who built the ark to save animals from the flood. Afterwards God made a promise to Noah and the animals: "Behold I establish my covenant with you and your descendants after you, and with every living creature that is with you, the birds, the cattle, and every beast of the earth with you, as many as came out of the ark" *(Genesis 9:9-10)*. God promised He would never again destroy the world with a flood.

MIXED-UP STORY

Unscramble the parts of this story. What did Lisa do first, second, third, etc.?

a. Lisa ate some bacon and eggs.

b. Lisa drove with her family to church.

c. Lisa washed and dressed.

d. Lisa went to Sunday school with her brother.

e. Lisa awoke as the clock rang at 8:00.

(*Answer:* e, c, a, b, d)

ANIMAL PROJECT

Draw animals mentioned in the Bible or cut out pictures of them. You could draw Daniel and the lions; Jesus riding a donkey; or Adam and Eve with the snake. Make these into a small booklet, with one picture on each page (or person and animal on facing pages).

You may want to tell a short story about each picture or pair of pictures.

Daniel and the lions, *Daniel 6:16;* Jesus riding the donkey, *Matthew 21:1-9;* Adam and Eve with the serpent (snake), *Genesis 3:1-6.*

(The Bible references are to help you tell a story for each picture.)

POPSICLE RECIPE

WHOLESOME POPS ON A SUMMER DAY

In your blender combine: 1 pint chocolate (or other flavor of) ice cream;

One cup of chocolate milk;

1/2 of a six-ounce can (1/3 cup) of *frozen* orange juice concentrate, *thawed;*

1/4 cup of powdered sugar.

Cover and blend until the mixture is smooth;

Pour the mixture into 10 three-ounce waxed paper drinking cups, filling each cup about 1/3 full;

Place in freezer;

When mixture is partially frozen, insert wooden sticks;

Freeze until firm.

To serve, peel off paper cup.

Serves 10 children!!! Have tasty fun!

JULY

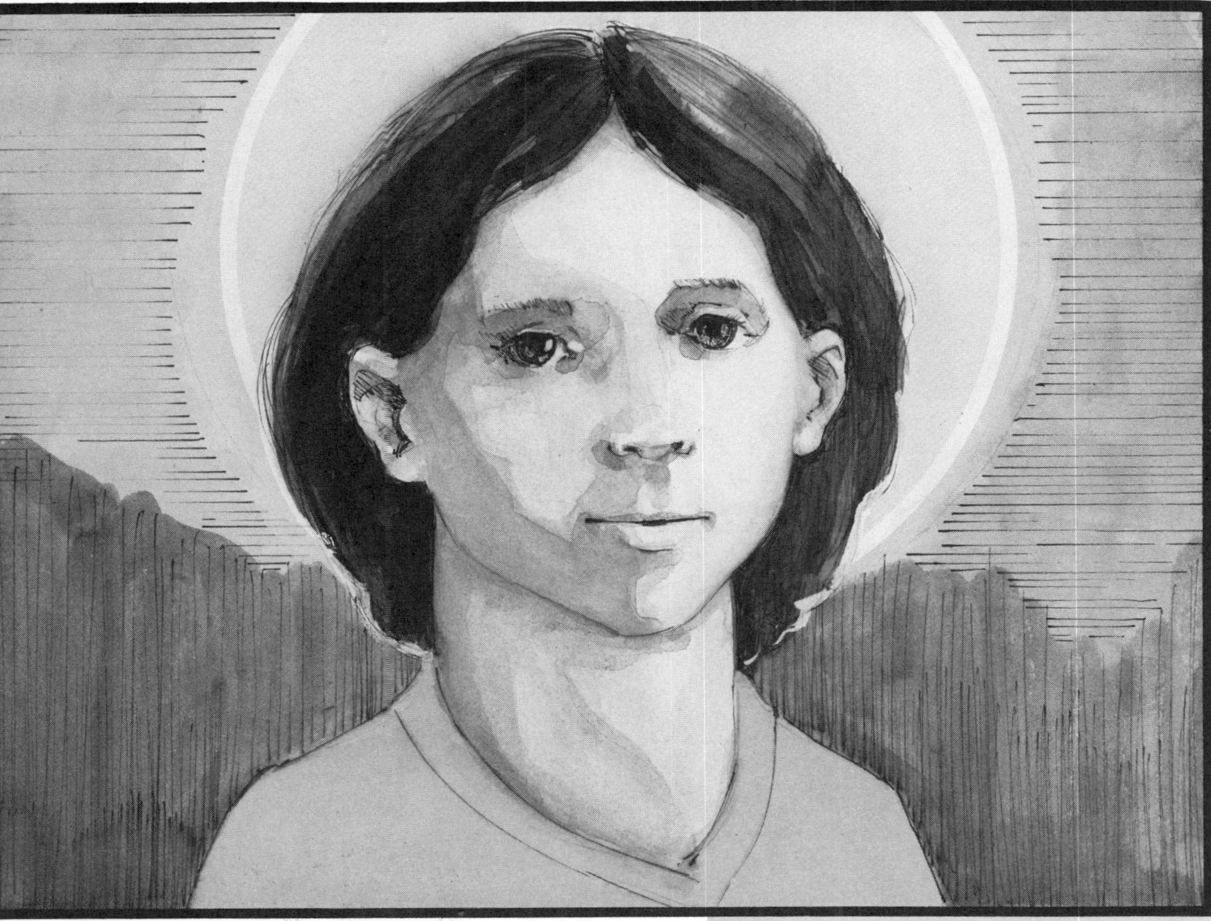

CHILDREN

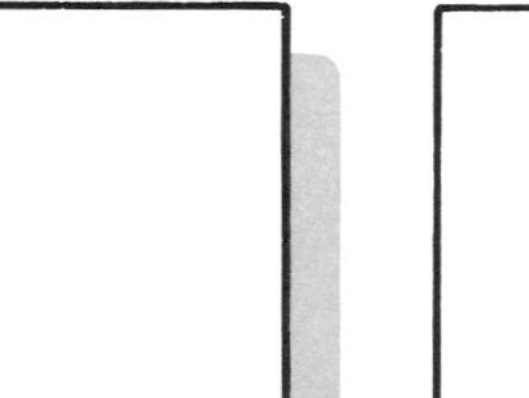
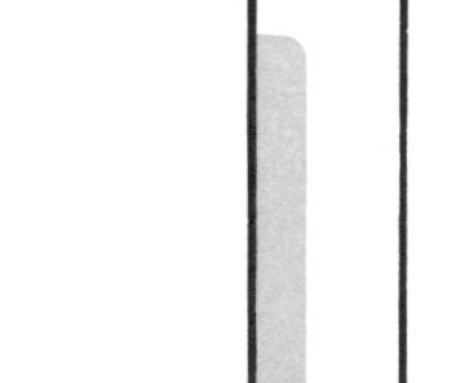

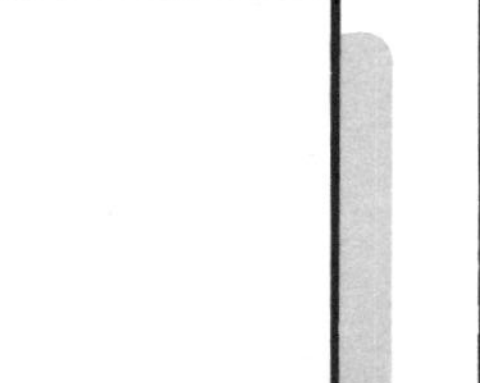
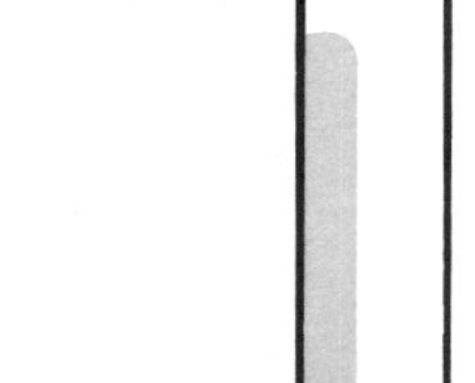
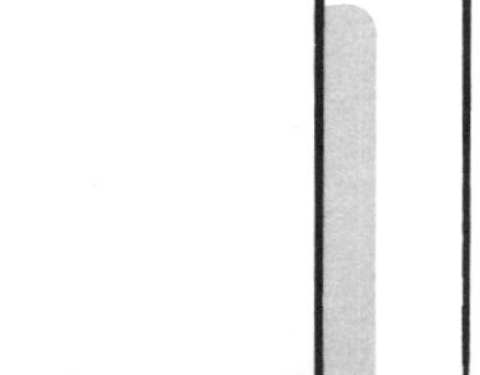
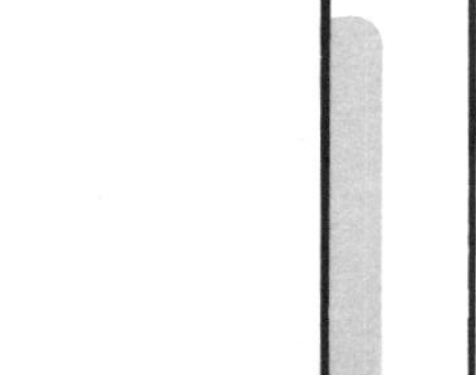

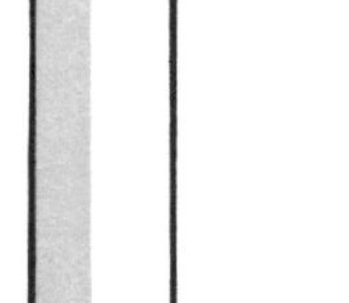
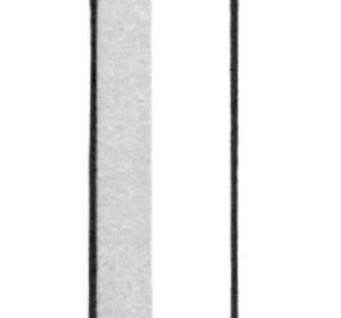
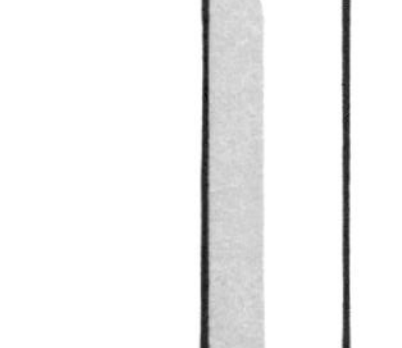
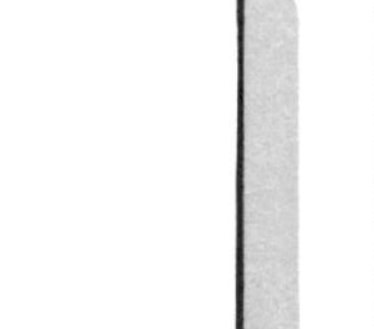

JULY

BIRTHSTONE:

Ruby

FLOWER:

Larkspur

BIRTHDATES OF PRESIDENTS/ FAMOUS PEOPLE

Calvin Coolidge
Born: July 4, 1872

John Quincy Adams
Born: July 11, 1767

Nathaniel Hawthorne
(American author)
Born: July 4, 1804

Amelia Earhart
(Early woman aviator)
Born: July 10, 1898

Henry D. Thoreau
(American author and nature-lover)
Born: July 12, 1817

	1st WEEK	2nd WEEK	3rd WEEK	4th WEEK	5th WEEK
SUNDAY					
MONDAY					
TUESDAY					
WEDNESDAY					

AMERICAN INDEPENDENCE DAY—JULY 4

The day of American independence began July 4, 1776. It has been celebrated each year since. The U.S.A. is now in its third century of independence.

The month of July was named after Julius Caesar.

THURSDAY					
FRIDAY					
SATURDAY					

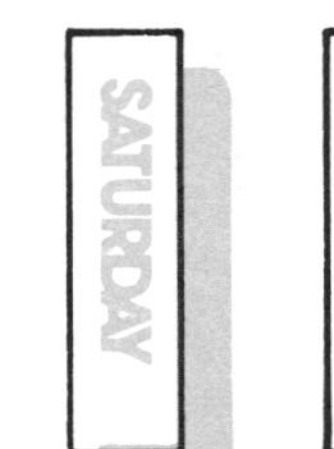
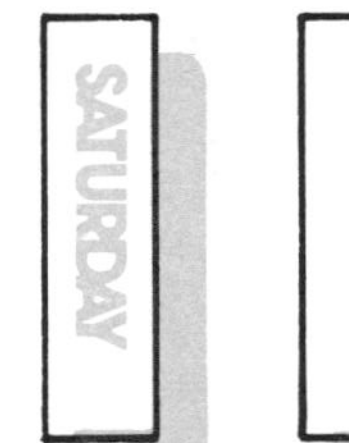

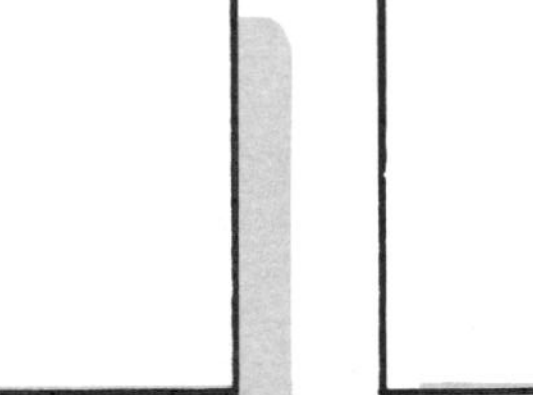

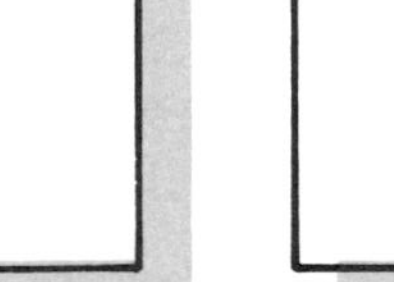
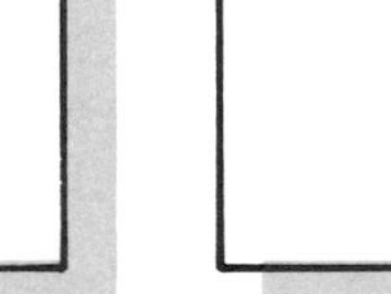

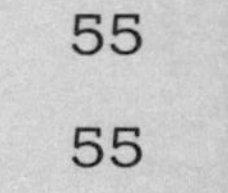
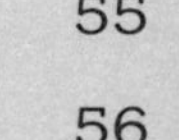

THINGS TO DO–

CHILDREN

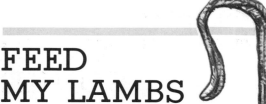

FEED MY LAMBS

"When they had finished breakfast, Jesus said to Simon Peter, 'Simon, son of John, do you love Me more than these?' He said to Him, 'Yes, Lord; You know that I love You.' He said to him, 'Feed My lambs.' A second time He said to him, 'Simon, son of John, do you love Me?' He said to Him, 'Yes, Lord, You know that I love You.' He said to him, 'Tend My sheep.' He said to him the third time, 'Simon, son of John, do you love Me?' Peter was grieved because He said to him the third time, 'Do you love Me?' And he said to Him, 'Lord, You know everything; You know that I love You.' Jesus said to him, 'Feed My sheep.'"

(John 21:15-17)

Jesus was testing the love and loyalty of Simon Peter in this passage. Are your love and loyalty sometimes tested? Do you love Jesus enough to be loyal to Him all your life?

KNOW YOUR BIBLE WORDS

Place the correct word from the box in front of the description below.

WORD BOX

Sorcerer	Caravan	Hallelujah	Zeus
Apostle	The Psalms	Ten Commandments	

______________ A group of people traveling together, especially traders with pack animals. Routes crisscrossed the ancient world, and cargo was often spices *(Genesis 37:25).*

______________ Chief of the Greek gods in New Testament times *(Acts 14:12-13).*

______________ "Messenger" or ambassador. In the Gospels, the 12 disciples of Jesus *(Mark 6:30).*

______________ An exclamation meaning "Praise the Lord!" Used in the Book of Revelation.

______________ One who practiced magic, or who divined, especially under the influence of potions *(Exodus 22:18).*

______________ Basic requirements of the covenant between God and His people *(Exodus 34:28).*

______________ Old Testament book made up of several collections of poems and songs for use in worship.

ABOUT CHILDREN

Discuss these passages with your parents and with other children, and see what you can learn from them.

"Do not withhold discipline from a child."

(Proverbs 23:13)

"And calling to Him a child, He put him in the midst of them and said, 'Truly, I say to you, unless you turn and become like children, you will never enter the kingdom of heaven. Whoever humbles himself like this child, he is the greatest in the kingdom of heaven.'"

(Matthew 18:2-4)

"And the Child Jesus grew and became strong, filled with wisdom; and the favor of God was upon Him."

(Luke 2:40)

"When I was a child, I spoke like a child, I thought like a child, I reasoned like a child; when I became a man, I gave up childish ways."

(1 Corinthians 13:11)

"If you then, who are evil, know how to give good gifts to your children, how much more will your Father who is in heaven give good things to those who ask Him!"

(Matthew 7:11)

"Train up a child in the way he should go, and when he is old he will not depart from it."

(Proverbs 22:6)

MAKE A BIBLE ANIMAL MERRY-GO-ROUND—A MOBILE

YOU WILL NEED:

Aluminum foil; string; cardboard and crayons; heavy straws; needle; glue.

Form a circle of foil about one-quarter inch thick.

Pull thread through the center with a needle.

Tie thread off on bottom of foil circle.

Remove needle and leave string there for the present.

(It will later be used for hanging.)

Glue four to eight straws evenly around the circle.

(Be sure glue dries well.)

Tie strings from ends of straws for hanging your animals on.

Cut out animals from Sunday school leaflets or coloring books and color them with crayons.

Put the string into the back of each animal with the needle, and tie it. (You could also glue the string instead.)

Now hang your mobile.

WEATHER WHEEL

Cut out paper clouds, snowflakes, raindrops, sun (or other weather symbols).

Arrange them around the inside of a paper plate (about 8"—10" in diameter), and glue them on.

Cut an arrow from construction paper; fasten it to the center of the plate with a two-pronged brass fastener.

At the top, punch a hole and string yarn through it.

Hang up and use it to show the weather each day. (Do it before you leave for school or Sunday school, or go out to play each day.)

Keep a record of the sunny and rainy days during your summer vacation; then use the wheel in fall and winter to show snowy days too. At the end of the year you might want to do some adding to find out how many days were rainy, or sunny, or snowy.

PRAYER ON THE FOURTH OF JULY

PRAYER ON FOURTH OF JULY

This is the birthday of our land;
May all her days be in God's hand.

May all her ways between the seas
Be ways of quietness and peace.

May her good flag shine high and bright,
May all the nations trust its light.

For peace and blessing may she stand,
America our land!

by Nancy Byrd Turner

(From *The Year Around: Poems for Children* by Alice Hazeltine and Elva S. Smith; Abingdon Press, 1956.

MAKE LUNCH FOR SOMEONE SPECIAL

The Bible tells us there is a right time for everything, including different kinds of weather.

"For everything there is a season and a time for every matter under heaven: a time to be born, and a time to die; a time to plant, and a time to pluck up what is planted; a time to kill, and a time to heal; a time to break down, and a time to build up a time to weep, and a time to laugh; a time to mourn, and a time to dance; a time to cast away stones, and a time to gather stones together; a time to embrace, and a time to refrain from embracing; a time to seek, and a time to lose; a time to keep, and a time to cast away; a time to rend, and a time to sew; a time to keep silence, and a time to speak; a time to love, and a time to hate; a time for war, and a time for peace."

(Ecclesiastes 3:2-8)

The Bible has many references to seasons and weather.

"While the earth remains, seedtime and harvest, cold and heat, summer and winter, day and night, shall not cease."

(Genesis 8:22)

"But I say to you, Love your enemies and pray for those who persecute you, so that you may be sons of your Father who is in heaven; for He makes His sun rise on the evil and on the good, and sends rain on the just and on the unjust."

(Matthew 5:45)

What does this passage tell you about the kind of person God is?

Talk about how the Lord provides rain and sun, and how these affect plants, grain, and all life.

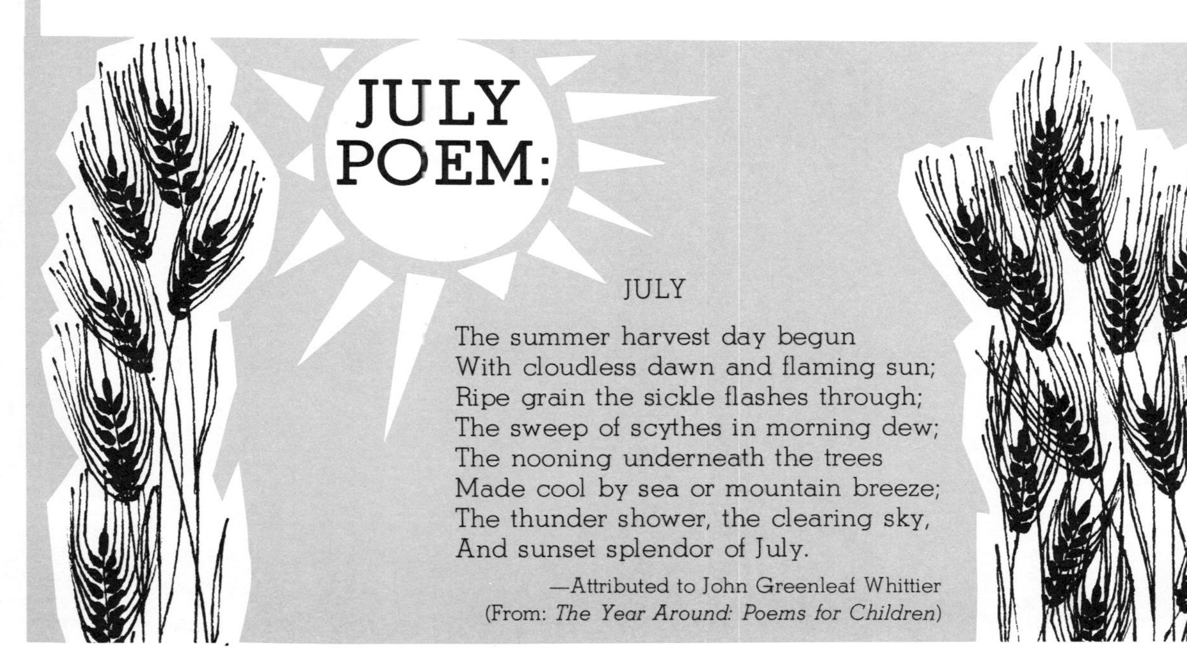

JULY POEM:

JULY

The summer harvest day begun
With cloudless dawn and flaming sun;
Ripe grain the sickle flashes through;
The sweep of scythes in morning dew;
The nooning underneath the trees
Made cool by sea or mountain breeze;
The thunder shower, the clearing sky,
And sunset splendor of July.

—Attributed to John Greenleaf Whittier
(From: *The Year Around: Poems for Children*)

Have a cookout for your Sunday school class, other friends, or your family.

Fix "Pigs-in-a-Blanket," potato chips, and lemonade.

To make pigs-in-a-blanket: Follow directions on the Bisquick package; roll the dough into a rectangle, about ¼" thick; cut these into 3" x 4" oblong pieces; wrap each piece of dough around a hot dog. Bake in oven 15 minutes at 450 degrees F.

CRAZY MIXED-UP LETTERS

Arrange the letters spelling "God," "Jesus," "Christ," "Mary," "Bible," and so on in a random or mixed-up order, as in the diagram below.

Ask your brother or sister or a friend to arrange the letters so they will be in the correct order.

D G O ___ ___ ___

R C H T S I ___ ___ ___ ___ ___ ___

S U E S J ___ ___ ___ ___ ___

Y A R M ___ ___ ___ ___

I L B E B ___ ___ ___ ___ ___

Add other crazy mixed-up words that you think of.

LET'S GO FISHING!

YOU WILL NEED:

2-4 horseshoe magnets;
foil or construction paper
paper clips;
twigs and strings;
a bowl of water.

YOU DO THIS:

1. Cut out fish shapes from the foil or paper;
2. Slide a paper clip onto each "fish";
3. Make your "fishing rod" by taping a piece of string onto a twig. Tie a horseshoe magnet to the end of the string;
4. Take turns fishing in a bowl of water (paper fish should be placed in a dry bowl), and see who can catch the most "fish."

RULE: One try per person for each turn.

If you make paper fish you can give each color a different value (so many points for white, red, etc.), and the winner is the one who gets the most points.

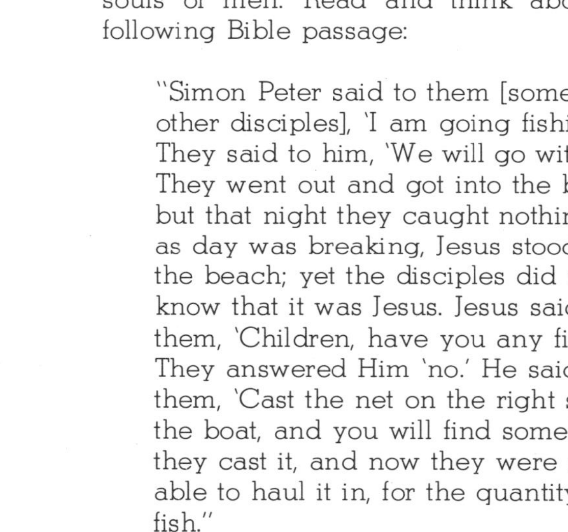

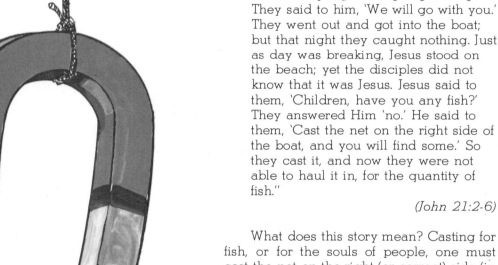

Jesus taught His disciples to "fish" for the souls of men. Read and think about the following Bible passage:

> "Simon Peter said to them [some of the other disciples], 'I am going fishing.' They said to him, 'We will go with you.' They went out and got into the boat; but that night they caught nothing. Just as day was breaking, Jesus stood on the beach; yet the disciples did not know that it was Jesus. Jesus said to them, 'Children, have you any fish?' They answered Him 'no.' He said to them, 'Cast the net on the right side of the boat, and you will find some.' So they cast it, and now they were not able to haul it in, for the quantity of fish."
>
> *(John 21:2-6)*

What does this story mean? Casting for fish, or for the souls of people, one must cast the net on the right (or correct) side (in the right way). "Fishing the way Jesus tells us to 'fish' brings results!"

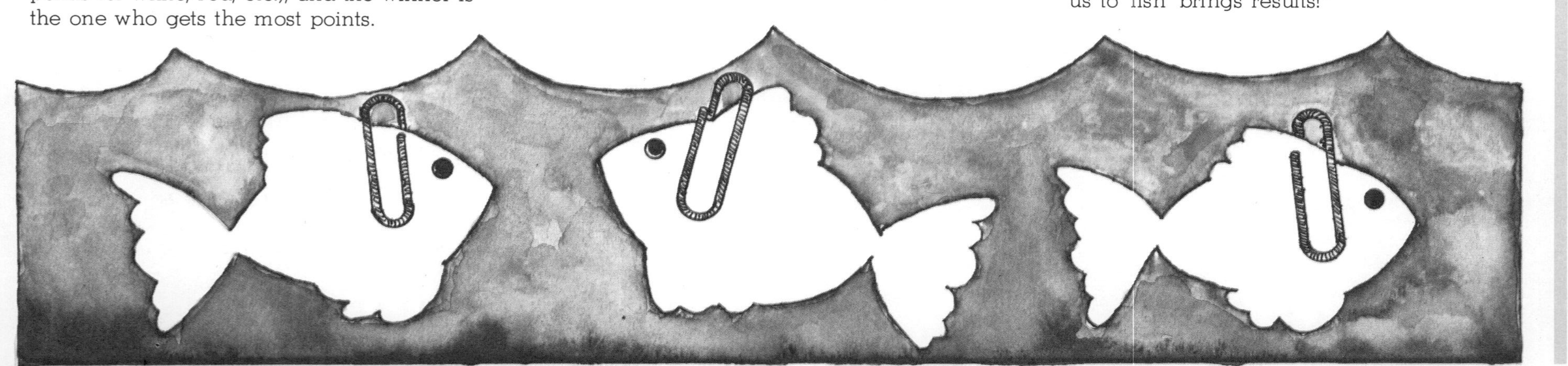

AUGUST

THE ENJOYMENT OF THE BIBLE

AUGUST

	1st WEEK	2nd WEEK	3rd WEEK	4th WEEK	5th WEEK
SUNDAY					
MONDAY					
TUESDAY					
WEDNESDAY					

BIRTHSTONE:

Peridot

This precious stone is the symbol of persuasiveness (persuading, convincing others of your viewpoint).

FLOWER:

Poppy

This is a beautiful flower, sometimes red, sometimes yellow, white, or violet; the head of the flower seems to nod. The poppy is the California State flower.

BIRTHDATES OF PRESIDENTS/ FAMOUS PEOPLE:

Herbert Hoover
Born: Aug. 10, 1874

Benjamin Harrison
Born: Aug. 20, 1833

Lyndon B. Johnson
Born: Aug. 27, 1908

Orville Wright
(With brother, Wilbur, made first successful airplane flight)
Born: Aug. 12, 1871

Alfred Lord Tennyson
(Writer)
Born: Aug. 20, 1809

In August 1456 the Gutenberg Bible was published.

Aug. 14, 1941, marks the "Atlantic Charter Day," which is significant because of the meeting between President Franklin D. Roosevelt and England's Prime Minister Winston Churchill on a warship, where they discussed peace.

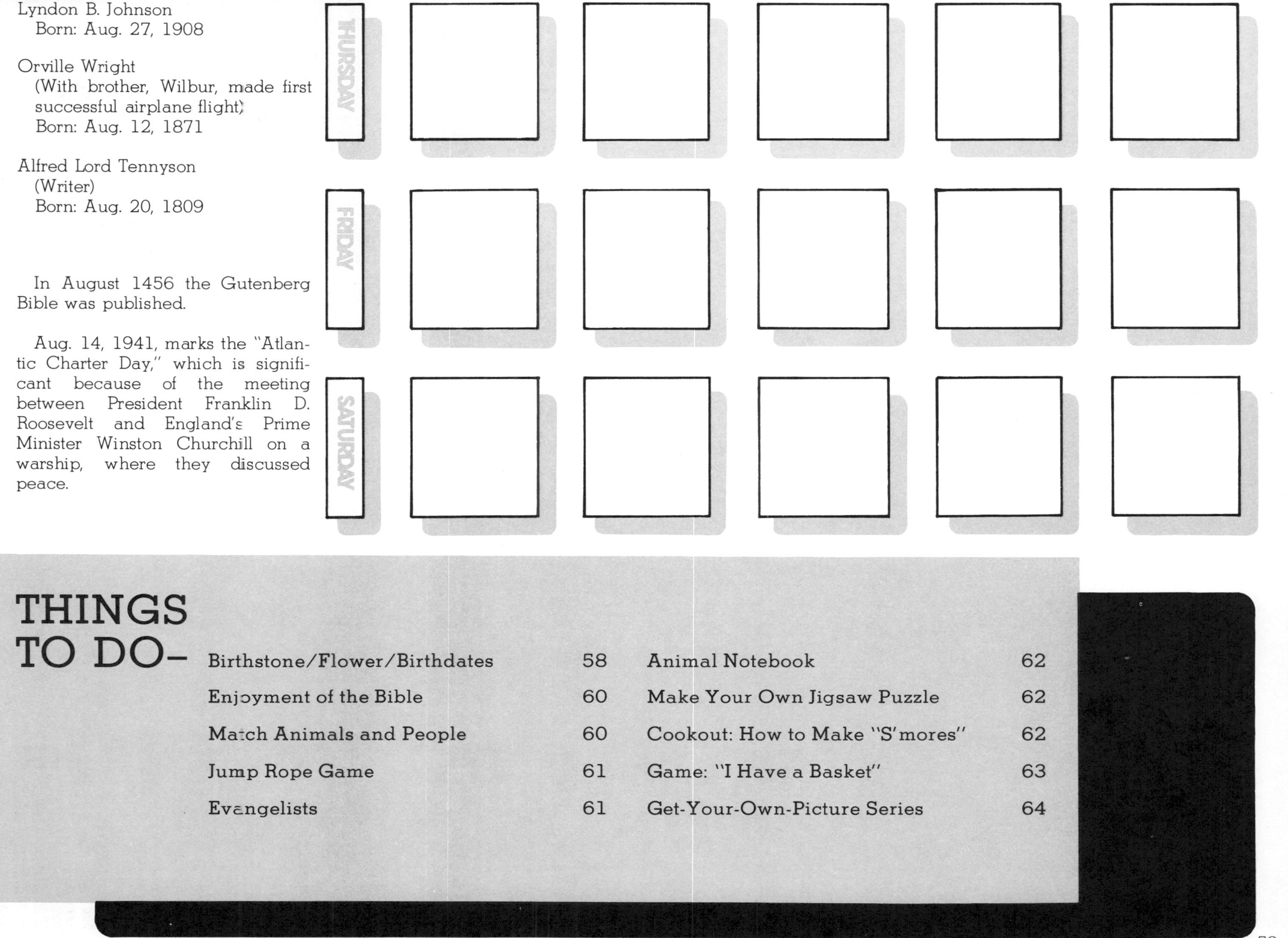

THINGS TO DO–

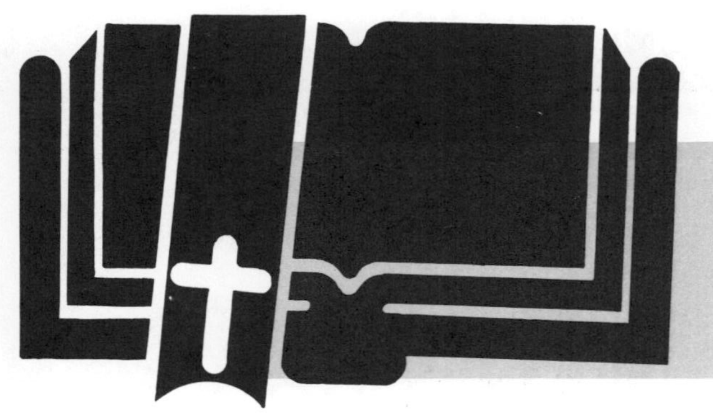

THE ENJOYMENT OF THE BIBLE

THE ENJOYMENT OF THE BIBLE

First, notice how many books are contained in the Old Testament. The first book is Genesis, which tells the story of Creation. Can you remember the names of some of the Old Testament books? Notice which books give the author's name and which don't.

MATCH ANIMALS AND PEOPLE IN THE BIBLE

As you work on this matching game, think of the poet Browning's statement: *"God made all creatures, gave them our love and our fear. To give sign, we and they are the children, one family here."*

Match up the animals associated with the people in the Bible:

A. DANIEL	a. Daniel 6:16	A. ______	SERPENT 1.
B. BALAAM	b. Numbers 22:21	B. ______	SWINE 2.
C. EVE	c. Genesis 3:1	C. ______	DOVE 3.
D. NOAH	d. Genesis 8:8	D. ______	SHEEP 4.
E. ABRAHAM	e. Genesis 22:13	E. ______	ASS 5.
F. DAVID	f. 1 Samuel 16:11	F. ______	COCK 6.
G. ELIJAH	g. 1 Kings 17:6	G. ______	LION 7.
H. JONAH	h. Jonah 1:17	H. ______	RAM 8.
I. PRODIGAL SON	i. Luke 15:15	I. ______	RAVENS 9.
J. PETER	j. Luke 22:34	J. ______	GREAT FISH 10.

(**Answers:** A, 7; B, 5; C, 1; D, 3; E, 8; F, 4; G, 9; H, 10; I, 2; J, 6)

Second, look at all the books of the New Testament. How many are there? The first four books are the Gospels: Matthew, Mark, Luke, and John. They tell about the life of Jesus. Acts tells how the Christian church got started. Most of the others are "epistles" (letters) written by the apostles to different churches. If you read a chapter a day, you can begin to know the Bible better, and God will speak to you through His Word.

JUMP ROPE GAME

LEARN A NEW JUMP-ROPE GAME.

Teach your younger brother or sister or neighbor a new jump-rope game to help pass the long summer days. Here's how to play the "best friend" game. You say: "I call in my very best friend and that is __________(name of player). One, two, three!"

As you say "three," your very best friend jumps into the rope with you, facing you. Jump to a rhyme that you like two or three times; then the friend jumps out as you continue to swing the rope and jump.

Now invite another friend, using the same words. After you have gone through all your friends, let one of them take over the rope jumping and do the same with several children.

EVANGELISTS

This puzzle will help you learn the names of the first four books of the Bible. Pick the names of the four evangelists from the letters below.

M	Q	S	T	N	V	W
A	A	O	H	A	B	Y
R	C	T	L	J	Z	C
K	E	S	T	O	B	G
C	K	J	R	H	G	H
D	U	V	T	N	E	L
O	L	N	M	B	K	W

Answer:
(Luke, John
Matthew, Mark)

ANIMAL NOTEBOOK

Make yourself an unusual notebook. You'll need: Cardboard; scissors; pencil; crayons or magic markers; writing paper, and brass fasteners.

Draw an animal—how about an elephant?—on a piece of cardboard about 6" wide and 4" high. Cut it out.

Take several sheets of paper; fold in half.

Lay the cutout animal on top of the folded sheets.

Trace around the animal. Cut all the sheets of paper in the same shape.

Fasten the sheets together at the fold.

Now you have an animal notebook. Write some secrets in it.

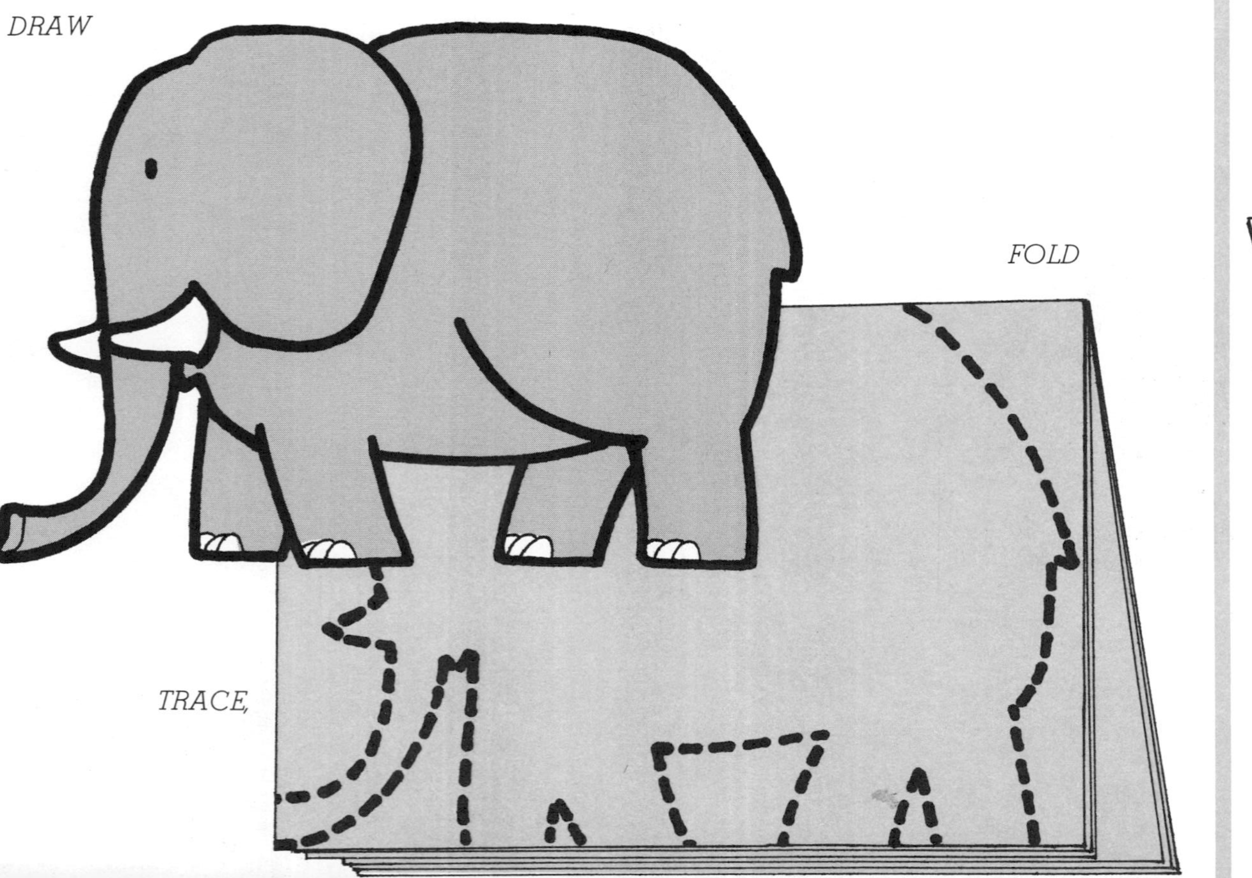

MAKE YOUR OWN JIGSAW PUZZLE

Paste a picture from your Sunday school lesson to a piece of cardboard. Make sure the picture and the cardboard are the same size. Turn the picture over and draw puzzle shapes. Then cut along the lines you drew. Scramble your pieces and try putting the puzzle back together.

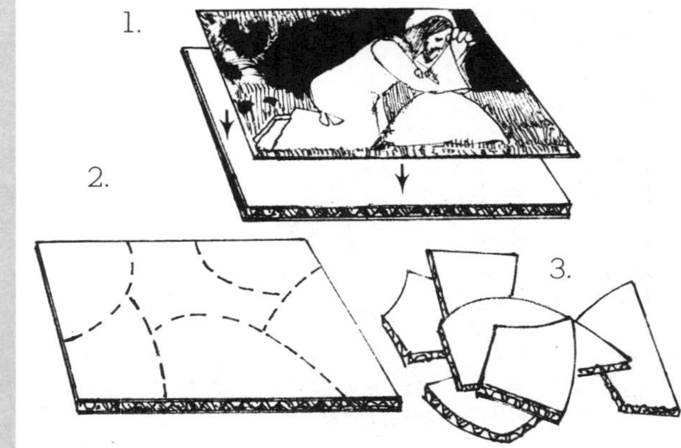

You could make many different jigsaw puzzles. Take them with you to Sunday school, give one to a friend on his or her birthday, or use to illustrate Bible stories in Sunday school.

COOKOUT: HOW TO MAKE "S'MORES"

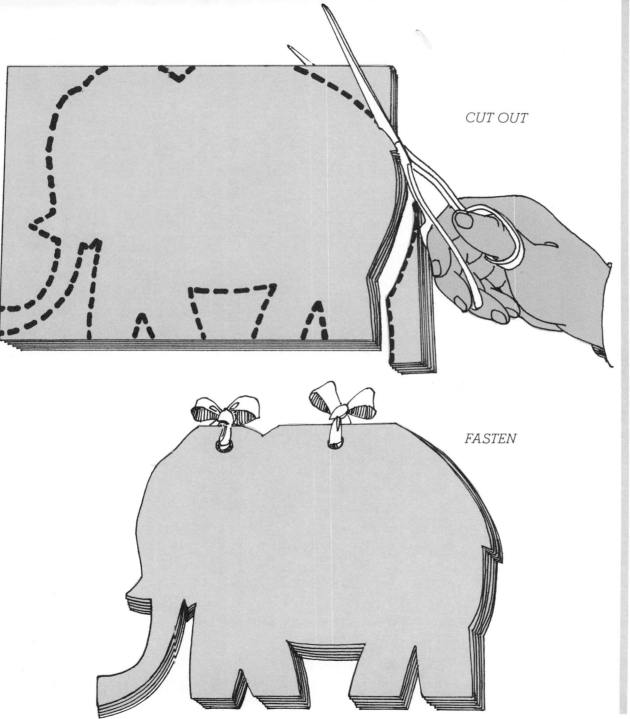

CUT OUT

FASTEN

August is a good month for a cookout. Help your mother or father by making the dessert.

You'll need: Chocolate bars, graham crackers, and marshmallows.

Directions:

Toast marshmallows in the fire. (Be careful that they are not burned up or charcoaled!) Place ½ of the chocolate bar on ½ of a graham cracker. Put a toasted marshamallow on top, and cover it with the other ½ of the graham cracker. Now you've made "s'mores."

GAME: "I HAVE A BASKET"

This is the way you play it: One player says, "I have a basket" (or bag, wagon, etc.). The next player says, "What's in it?"

The first person mentions some objects beginning with the letter *A* (apples, avocados, etc.). The next player then says, "I have a basket" and when he is asked what's in it, he mentions an object or article beginning with the letter *B*.
The players go through the whole alphabet this way.
(To test your knowledge of the Bible, play an alternate form of this game by using only Biblical names (A, Adam; B, Benjamin; C, Christ, etc.).

GET-YOUR-OWN-PICTURE SERIES

(A "MOVIE" OF YOUR GROWTH)

Ask you parents for old snapshots of yourself (or a sister or brother).

Cut the edges off each picture so it is the same size as a sheet of small tablet paper, about 3" x 5". (Smaller ones are too hard to use properly; larger ones may not be needed.)

Glue each picture onto a sheet of paper. If you have 5 or 10 pictures, you will need 5 or 10 sheets of paper to make your "movie."

After you have every picture glued to a single sheet of paper, arrange the sheets in a "book." Fasten one end with two-pronged brass fasteners.

Hold the fastened end of the book in your left hand and flip the pages, as you would the pages of a regular book, to see your pictures "fly" by. This makes time "fly," and shows how you have grown from a baby to your present size. Now you have a "movie" of your growth.

Not only do your looks change, you grow in other ways too.
Discuss the following passages about spiritual growth:

"And the child grew and became strong, filled with wisdom; and the favor of God was upon Him."

(Luke 2:40)

"Rather, speaking the truth in love, we are to grow up in every way into Him who is the Head, into Christ, from whom the whole body, joined and knit together by every joint with which it is supplied, when each part is working properly, makes bodily growth and upbuilds itself in love."

(Ephesians 4:15-16)

SEPTEMBER

Religious News Service Photo

PARABLES OF THE BIBLE

SEPTEMBER

	1st WEEK	2nd WEEK	3rd WEEK	4th WEEK	5th WEEK
SUNDAY					
MONDAY					
TUESDAY					
WEDNESDAY					

BIRTHSTONE:

Sapphire

A precious gem, deep blue in color, and related to the ruby. It signifies clear thinking.

FLOWER:

Aster

Aster means "star," and the flower resembles a star. With a yellow disk, it has rays growing in all directions. These rays range in color from white, pale blue, or pink to darker blue.

SPECIAL EVENTS:

First U.S. newspaper
Sept. 1754

Orville Wright stayed in the air in his "flying machine" more than one hour.

BIRTHDATES OF PRESIDENTS/ FAMOUS PEOPLE:

William Howard Taft
Born: Sept. 15, 1857

Jane Adams
(Peace advocate; won Nobel Peace Prize, 1931)
Born: Sept. 6, 1869

O. Henry
(Writer)
Born: Sept. 10, 1862

THURSDAY

FRIDAY

SATURDAY

THINGS TO DO–

"CHILD OF GOD" MOBILE

The materials you will need to make this mobile are:

Regular coat hanger; string; yarn;

Your picture (maybe you'll want to mount it on cardboard);
Some good work papers from school; your favorite poem;
Several 3" x 5" cards with the following information:

A) The date of your baptism.
B) The name of your favorite hymn.
C) Your favorite Bible passage and where it is in the Bible.
D) Your favorite prayer (or the name of the prayer).
E) A drawing of your church.
F) The name of your Sunday school teacher.

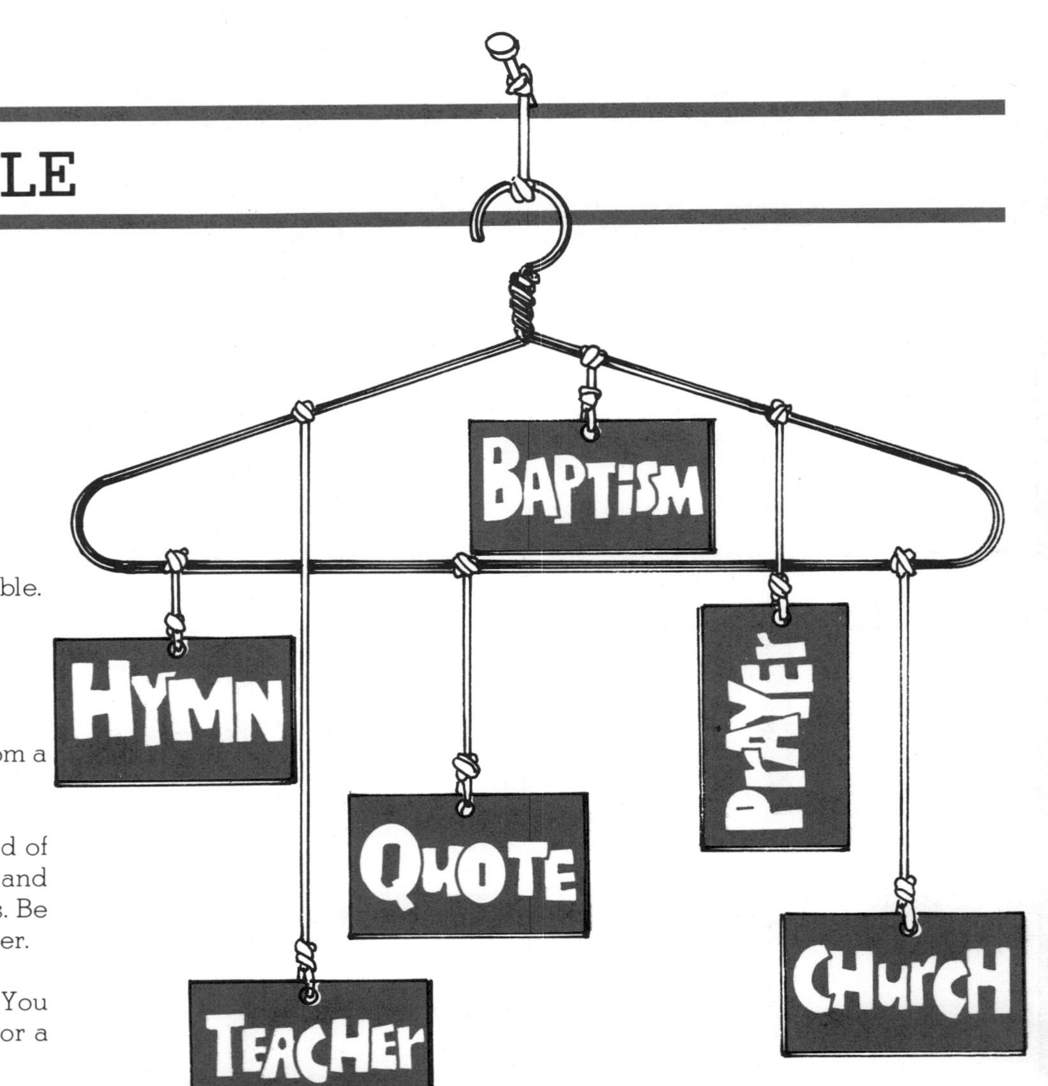

Tie a string or piece of yarn to the coat hanger. Then hang it from a door frame, the ceiling, or some other place in your room.

Get your picture and write your name on it. Then write "child of God" next to your name. Punch a hole in the picture, tie a string to it, and attach the string to the hanger. Do the same with all the other items. Be sure to balance them so they won't all slide to one side of the hanger.

Show your parents, brothers, or sisters what you have made. (You might want to make a mobile for someone else in the family or for a friend.)

THROUGH THE CHURCH YEAR

This month is a good time to discuss the main festivals of the church year, and to decide how your family will celebrate them.

ADVENT

During the four weeks of Advent we prepare our families for the coming of the birthday of Jesus. We greet Him with "O Come, O Come, Emmanuel" and "Hosanna to the Son of David." We can make or purchase an Advent wreath or an Advent calendar.

TWELVE DAYS
OF CHRISTMAS

Rather than limit activities to Christmas Eve and Christmas Day only, parents can help their children find new meanings and values in this festive time. If you are a "singing family," have all members of the family (and guests) join in the singing of hymns and carols every day or evening. If you are a "making family," you can paint a creche of plaster or ceramic, or even purchase molds for making the figures yourself. The family will treasure the creche for years to come.

Sewing sculpture is another popular craft.

If you are a "reading family," you can read stories about Christmas, as well as the Gospels.

EPIPHANY

Arise, shine! Your Light has come! Christ is come for the Gentiles—the Magi (Wise Men). Stars are a symbol for the "Light of the World" *(John 8:1)*. Straws can be cut, gathered, and fastened to form stars. White paper can be folded and cut out to form star-like snowflakes. On Epiphany, family gifts could be exchanged to remind everyone of the coming of the Wise Men to Bethlehem with their gifts.

LENT

Lent reminds us of Christ's war against Satan, the battle between good and evil. We can discuss events in the news and in our personal lives that show evil and sin. We can learn that "doing good" is doing God's will. Meditations, devotions, and readings from the Gospels at mealtime, with a cross in evidence, help to emphasize the theme of repentance. Palm Sunday (Triumphant Entry), Maundy Thursday (Last Supper), and Good Friday (Crucifixion) are each "special" days.

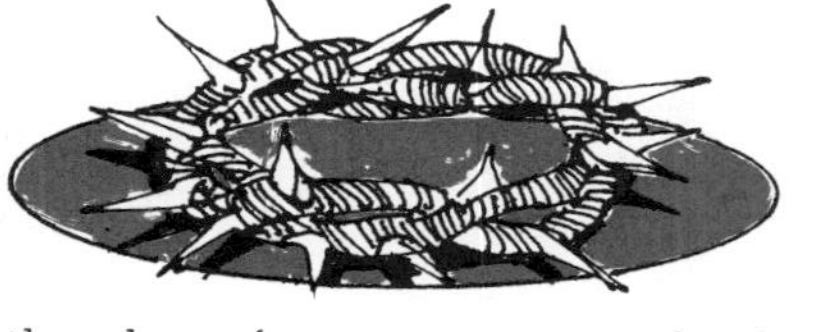

EASTER

This is the day of resurrection, rebirth, and renewal. "We have been born anew to a living hope through the resurrection of Jesus Christ from the dead" *(1 Peter 1:3)*. What Easter symbols do we have in our homes that represent rebirth? Flowers, eggs, butterflies. The six Sundays after Easter are a good time to discuss our rebirth in the risen Christ, our baptism, and Holy Communion.

ASCENSION

The Ascension of our Lord (40 days after Easter) is often ignored by many Christians. We confess (in the Apostles' Creed) that Christ "ascended into heaven and sitteth on the right hand of God the Father." This may be discussed with your children.

PENTECOST

Pentecost is often called the birthday of the Christian church. Through the months of Sundays after Pentecost, the family could discuss the gifts of the Spirit *(Galatians 5:22-23)*. A project could be a mobile made up of objects that represent these spiritual gifts: a heart for love, a smiling face for joy, a dove for peace, etc. Deciding what objects to use might stimulate some interesting discussions.

MAKE YOUR FAMILY OF GOD TREE

Every family has a "tree." The "tree" refers to your parents, your two sets of grandparents, and as far back as you want or can go.

You can draw a big tree on a large sheet of paper and paste on the various pictures. Or you can get a large piece of cloth (such as an old white tablecloth, about 2′ x 2′) and draw a tree on it with a magic marker or a crayon; then pin on the pictures of various family members.

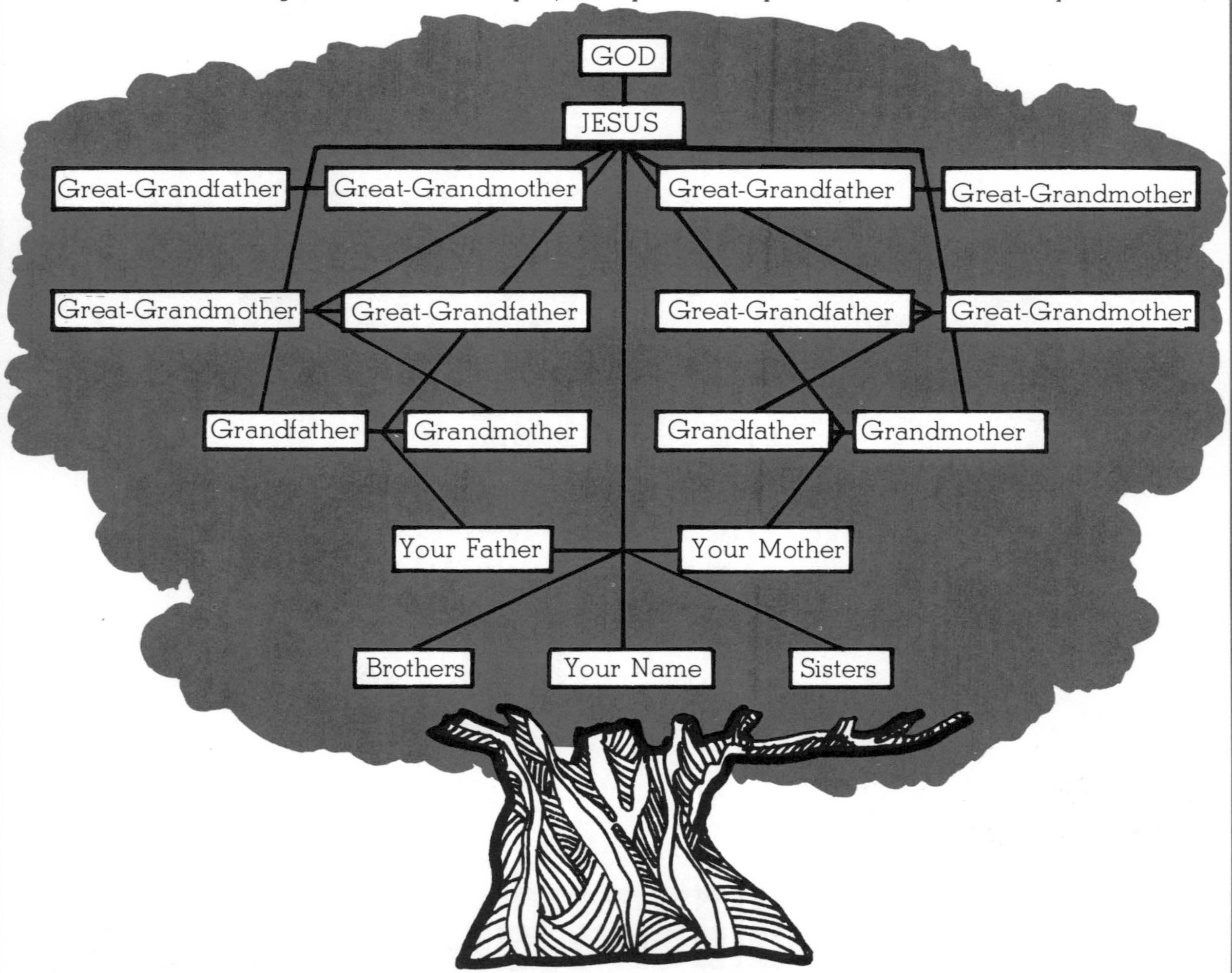

GOD

JESUS

Great-Grandfather — Great-Grandmother — Great-Grandfather — Great-Grandmother

Great-Grandmother — Great-Grandfather — Great-Grandfather — Great-Grandmother

Grandfather — Grandmother — Grandfather — Grandmother

Your Father — Your Mother

Brothers — Your Name — Sisters

FAMILY OF GOD TREE

APPLES

What a delicious fruit the apple is! Apples are plentiful in the fall. And there are so many, many things you can do with apples.
Here are some things you can make from apples:

apple pie	apple jelly
apple fritters	apple sauce
apple cider	apple dumplings

and so on.

Get a recipe book and look up one or more of these recipes. Surprise your parents, a neighbor, a friend, or a sick person with some really delicious "apple food."

There are many slogans and sayings about apples:

"An apple a day keeps the doctor away."

"You are the apple of my eye."

"Applesauce!" *(when you think someone is kidding you)*

PARABLES IN THE BIBLE

MAKE YOUR FAMILY TREE (ALTERNATIVE PLAN):

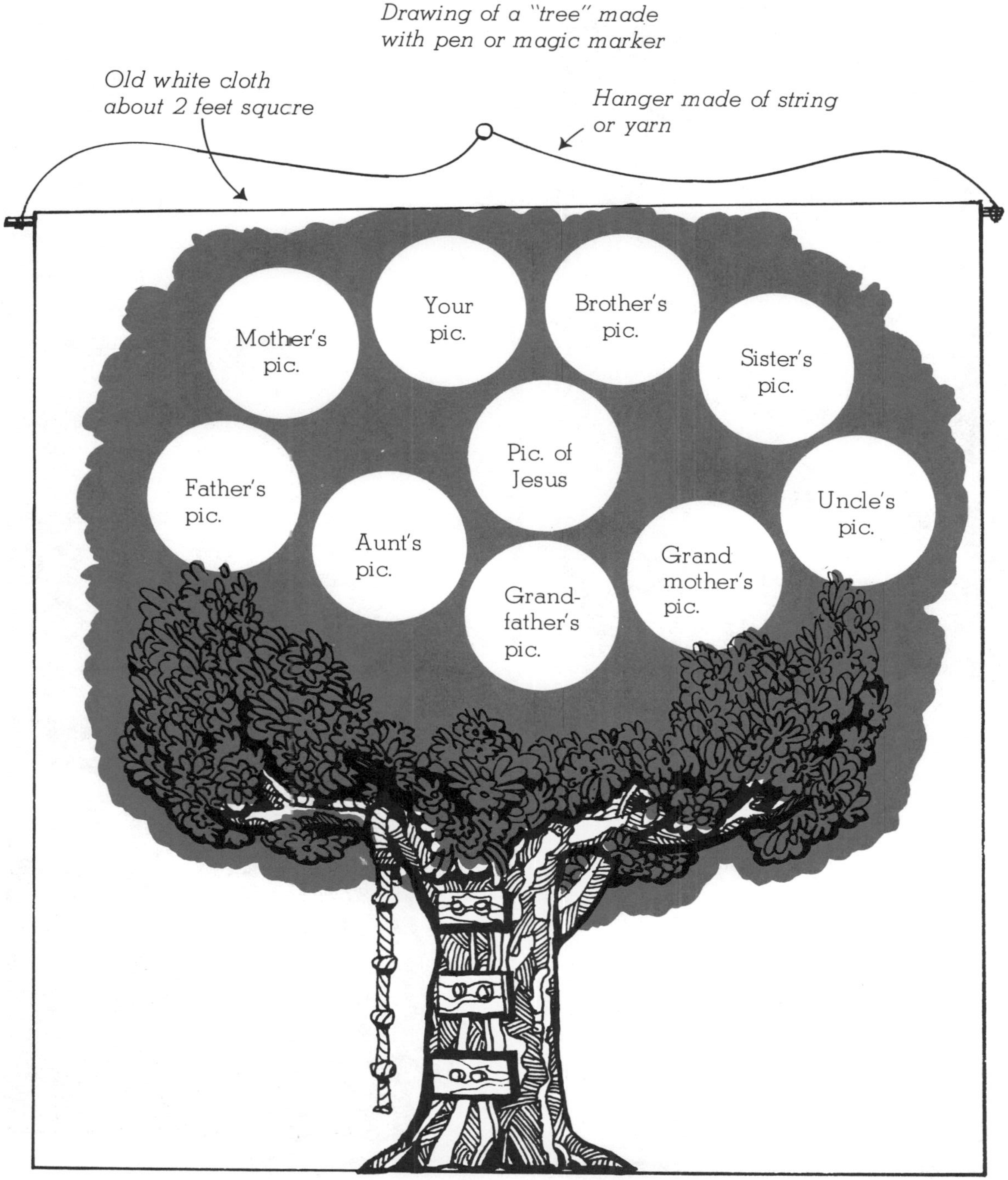

Drawing of a "tree" made with pen or magic marker

Old white cloth about 2 feet squcre

Hanger made of string or yarn

Mother's pic.

Your pic.

Brother's pic.

Sister's pic.

Father's pic.

Pic. of Jesus

Uncle's pic.

Aunt's pic.

Grand-father's pic.

Grand mother's pic.

Find several parables (stories) that Jesus told in the Gospels. Write them on cards or paper. If you do not know the meaning of any parable use the card as a reminder to ask your parents, your teacher, or pastor what Jesus wanted you to learn from His story.

"Hear then the parable of the sower. When any one hears the word of the kingdom and does not understand it, the evil one comes and snatches away what is sown in his heart; this is what was sown along the path. As for what was sown on rocky ground, this is he who hears the Word and immediately receives it with joy; yet he has no root in himself, but endures for a while, and when tribulation or persecution arises on account of the Word, immediately he falls away."

(Matthew 13:18-21)

"And again Jesus spoke to them in parables, saying, 'The kingdom of heaven may be compared to a king who gave a marriage feast for his son, and sent his servants to call those who were invited to the marriage feast; but they would not come. Again he sent other servants, saying, 'Tell those who are invited, Behold, I have made ready my dinner, my oxen and my fat calves are killed, and everything is ready; come to the marriage feast.' But they made light of it and went off, one to his farm, another to his business, while the rest seized his servants, treated them shamefully, and killed them. The king was angry, and he sent his troops and destroyed those murderers and burned their city."

(Matthew 22:2-7).

BOUQUET OF DRY FLOWERS

Get ready for fall and winter by collecting dry leaves and flowers to brighten someone's room.

You'll need: Flowers—marigolds, daisies, zinnias; string; scissors; and a coat hanger.

DIRECTIONS:
Take the leaves off the stems, but leave the stems intact.
Tie the flowers together at the end of the stems.
Tie the string onto a coat hanger with the flowers hanging upside-down.
Let the flowers dry for about a week or two in a dark, dry place like a closet.
Then take the flowers out of the closet, untie them, and arrange them in a vase. Be carefuly in handling them—they may be very dry and brittle.

A PRAYER FOR LITTLE THINGS

Please God, take care of little things
The fledglings that have not their wings,
Till they are big enough to fly
And stretch their wings across the sky.

And please take care of little seeds,
So small among the forest weeds,
Till they have grown as tall as trees
With heavy boughs, take care of these.

And please take care of drops of rain
Like beads upon a broken chain,
Till in some river in the sun
The many silver drops are one.

Take care of small new lambs that bleat,
Small foals that totter on their feet,
And all small creatures ever known
Till they are strong to stand alone.

And please take care of children who
Kneel down at night to pray to You,
Oh, please keep safe the little prayer
That like the big ones asks Your care.

by Eleanor Farjion
Houghton Mifflin Publ. Co., 1945

LABOR DAY POEM

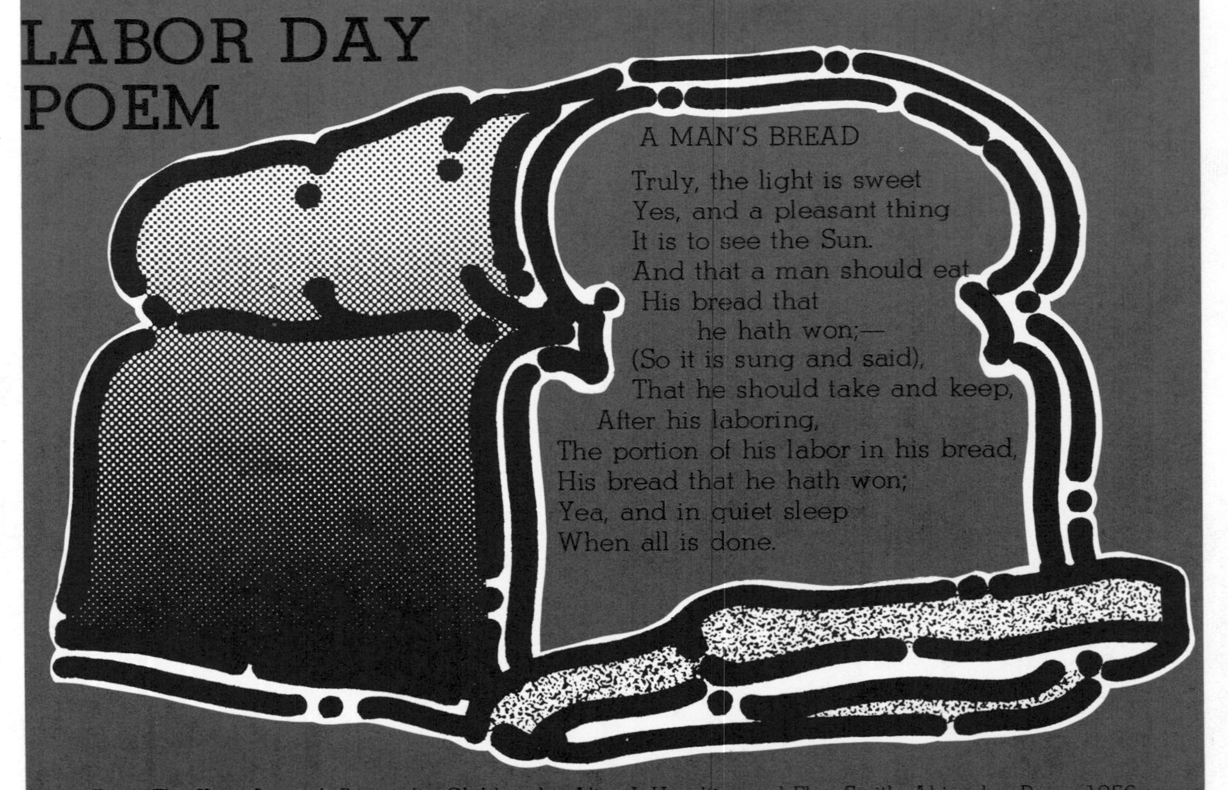

A MAN'S BREAD

Truly, the light is sweet
Yes, and a pleasant thing
It is to see the Sun.
And that a man should eat
His bread that
he hath won;—
(So it is sung and said),
That he should take and keep,
After his laboring,
The portion of his labor in his bread,
His bread that he hath won;
Yea, and in quiet sleep
When all is done.

From *The Year Around: Poems for Children* by Alice I. Hazeltire and Elva Smith. Abingdon Press, 1956.

OCTOBER

WHAT THE SCRIPTURES SAY ABOUT GOD

OCTOBER

BIRTHSTONE:

Opal

The opal is a brilliant jewel; it shines and twinkles because of the light reflected from the thousands of tiny cracks in the stone. Opals are fragile gems and must be handled carefully.

FLOWER:

Calendula

This flower is also known as the pot marigold because it can be added to a pot of stew for color and flavor. It is sometimes used in medicine for healing wounds.

BIRTHDATES OF PRESIDENTS/ FAMOUS PEOPLE:

Rutherford B. Hayes
Born: Oct. 4, 1822

Chester Arthur
Born: Oct. 5, 1830

Dwight D. Eisenhower
Born: Oct. 14, 1890

Theodore Roosevelt
Born: Oct. 27, 1858

	1st WEEK	2nd WEEK	3rd WEEK	4th WEEK	5th WEEK
SUNDAY					
MONDAY					
TUESDAY					
WEDNESDAY					

John Adams
Born: Oct. 30, 1735

Sarah Bernhardt
(Actress)
Born: Oct. 12, 1844

Mahatma Gandhi
(Indian religious leader)
Born: Oct. 15, 1869

John Keats
(English poet)
Born: Oct. 21, 1795

SPECIAL EVENTS:

First complete English Bible published Oct. 1535

President George Washington issued the first Thanksgiving proclamation Oct. 1789

Columbus Day Oct. 12

United Nations Day Oct. 24

Reformation Day Oct. 31

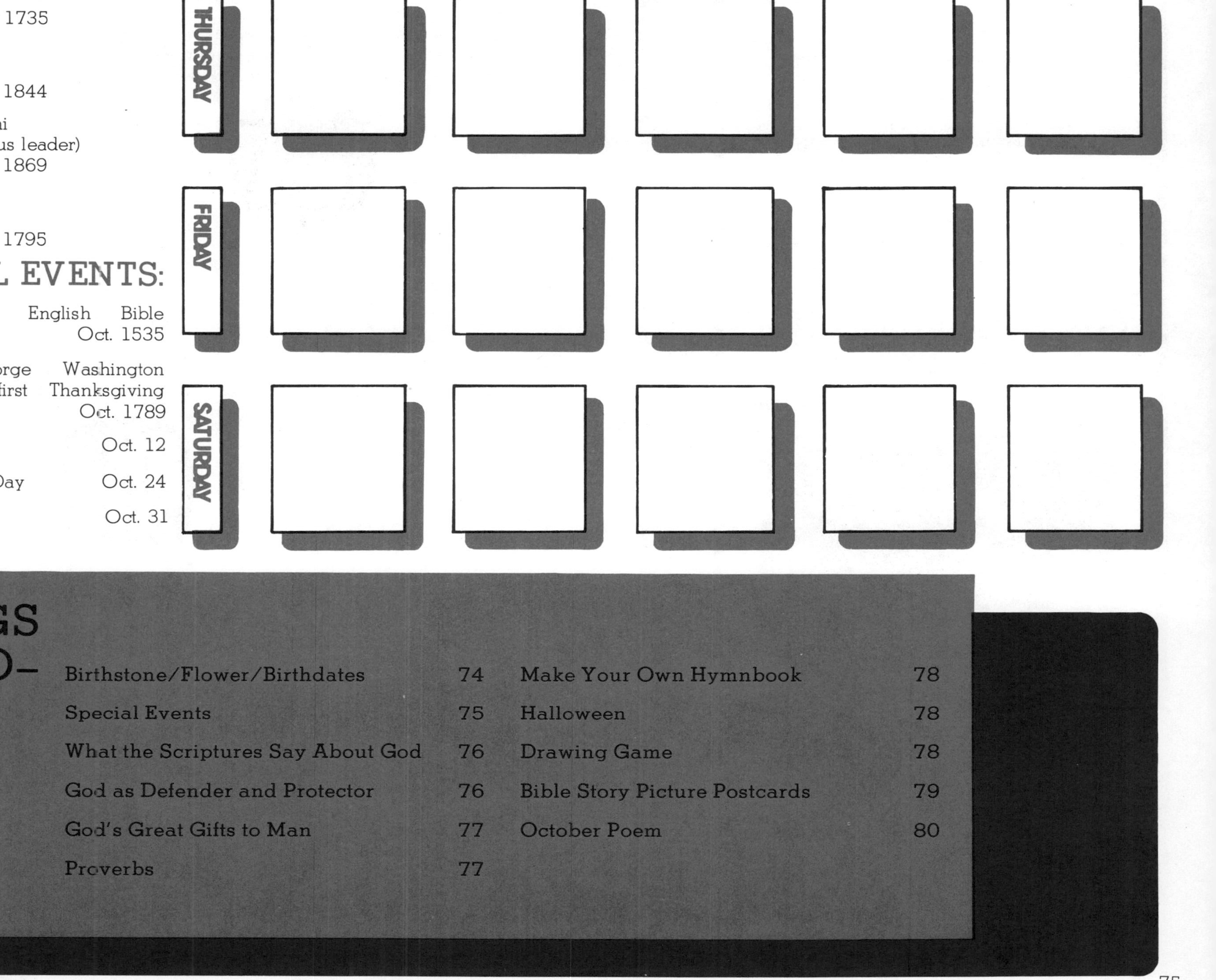

THINGS TO DO–

WHAT THE SCRIPTURES SAY ABOUT GOD

WHAT THE SCRIPTURES SAY ABOUT GOD

GOD AS CREATOR:

"When God began to form the universe, the world was void and vacant, darkness lay over the abyss; but the Spirit of God was hovering over the waters. God said, 'Let there be light,' and there was light."

(Genesis 1:1-3)

"Then God said, 'Let Us make man in Our image, after Our likeness; and let them have dominion over the fish of the sea, and over the birds of the air, and over the cattle, and over all the earth, and over every creeping thing that creeps upon the earth.'"

(Genesis 1:26)

GOD AS JUST AND MERCIFUL JUDGE

"Come, now, let us reason together, says the Lord; though your sins are like scarlet, they shall be as white as snow; though they are red like crimson, they shall become like wool. If you are willing and obedient, you shall eat the good of the land; but if you refuse and rebel, you shall be devoured by the sword; for the mouth of the Lord has spoken."

(Isaiah 1:18-20)

GOD AS DEFENDER AND PROTECTOR

A mighty fortress is our God.
A trusty shield and weapon;
He helps us free from ev'ry need
That hath us now o'ertaken.
The old evil foe
Now means deadly woe;
Deep guile and great might
Are his dread arms in fight;
On earth is not his equal.

Read Psalm 46

"For the Lord loves justice; He will not forsake his saints. The righteous shall be preserved forever, but the children of the wicked shall be cut off."

(Psalm 37:28)

GOD AS THE LOVING FATHER

"For the Father Himself loveth you, because ye have loved Me, and have believed that I came out from God. I came forth from the Father, and I came into the world: again I leave the world, and go to the Father."

(John 16:27-28)

GOD'S GREAT GIFTS TO MAN

What are God's greatest gifts to us? Try asking several people and then write down what they say. But before you ask others, write down what *you* think are the answers to this question.

Here are some *possible* answers. See what you think of them. If you like these answers, draw a picture of each one.

Water Man could not live long without water; neither could animals, plants, or trees.
(Draw a picture of a cool lake with shimmering water.)

Trees Trees give shade; provide beauty; can be sawed into lumber for homes and furniture.
(Draw several trees or a forest.)

Animals Animals provide food and companionship for people, and help us in other ways. Earth worms are tiny animals that aerate the soil so plants and trees can grow.
(Draw your favorite animals.)

Love Surely this is the greatest gift of all, for without love none of the others would mean much.

"For God so loved the world that He gave His only begotten Son, that whosoever believeth in Him should not perish, but have everlasting life."

(John 3:16)

(How would you draw "love"? Maybe a mother caring for a baby; a father walking hand-in-hand with a boy or girl.)

PROVERBS

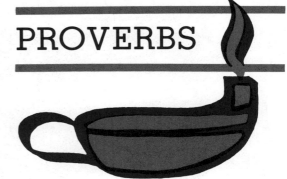

A proverb is a short, meaningful saying, often taken from the Bible or from ancient literature, that is a good guide to action. Here are some for you to remember and use.

- "A merry heart doeth good like a medicine."
  (Proverbs 17:22a).

- "A soft answer turneth away wrath; but grievous words stir up anger."
  (Proverbs 15:1)

- "A good name is rather to be chosen than great riches, and loving favor rather than silver and gold."
  (Proverbs 22:1)

- "Let another man praise thee, and not thine own mouth; a stranger and not thine own lips."
  (Proverbs 27:2)

- "A man that hath friends must show himself friendly."
  (Proverbs 18:24a)

You may want to write, print, or type these proverbs onto sheets of paper, bind them, and make a "Proverbs Book" out of them. Perhaps you will want to add more proverbs.

MAKE YOUR OWN HYMNBOOK

Pick several hymns from your hymnal and write (print, type) each one on a separate sheet of paper.

Fasten the sheets of paper together at one end (or one side), with two-pronged brass fasteners, making a "book."

Some hymns you might want to include are the following (but select as many of your own as you like):

"Onward Christian Soldiers"
"A Mighty Fortress Is Our God"
"Abide with Me"
"Alas and Did My Savior Bleed"
"Blest Be the Tie That Binds"
"God Be with You till We Meet Again"
"God Moves in a Mysterious Way"
"I Need Thee Every Hour"
"Jesus Calls Us o'er Tumult"
"Lead Kindly Light"
"Rock of Ages"
"What a Friend We Have in Jesus"

After you have made your own hymnbook, show it to your parents, grandparents, Sunday school teacher, and others.

HALLOWEEN

"Halloween" means "holy or hallowed evening," and comes on Oct. 31, immediately before All Saints' Day (Nov. 1).

A DRAWING GAME

Distribute a piece of paper (3" x 5" or 4" x 6") to each player. Each person in the group draws the head of a human, an animal, or a bird, and folds it over, leaving a mark where the neck begins. The folded paper is passed to the next player.

The next person draws a body and, folding it over, passes it to a third person, who draws legs.

Since no one knows exactly what the previous person (or persons) has drawn, the final result is very funny.

The whole drawing can be broken down into more parts (arms, hands, feet, etc.), and the results will be even funnier!

As Christianity spread throughout Europe in the seventh and eighth centuries A.D., it was considered important to have an All Saints' Day. Originally the ceremonies on what is now known as Halloween were to drive out evil spirits, and to remind people not to sell themselves to the devil.

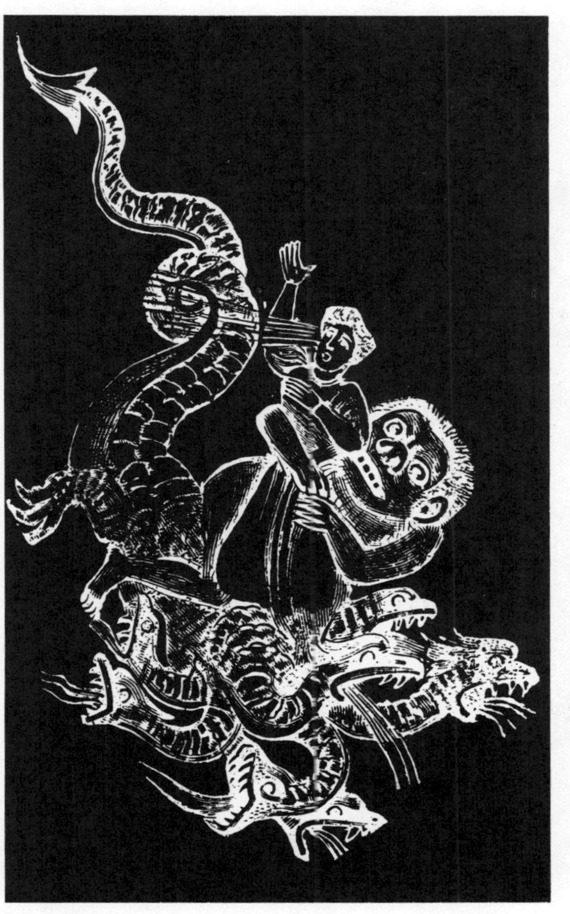

As time passed, the purpose of All Saints' Day was partly forgotten. It became a day to celebrate bountiful harvests and get ready for winter. But faint memories still linger. Perhaps today when children wear masks, ghost costumes, and witches' hats, they are unconsciously re-enacting those ancient ceremonies to drive out evil spirits.

BIBLE STORY PICTURE POSTCARDS

Remember the postcards you made in June? Oct. 25 is the anniversary of the first postcards sent in the United States mail (in 1870).

Make some postcards with your favorite Bible story pictures or drawings (the way you did in June) and send them to friends. (You can put a stamp on them and mail them, or you can give them to friends when you see them.)

Here are some pictures or drawings you might use:

a) Jesus preaching to crowds of people;
b) Jesus blessing the children;
c) Drawing of the Bible;
d) Jesus on the cross (or a drawing of just a cross);
e) A church with worshipers walking in.

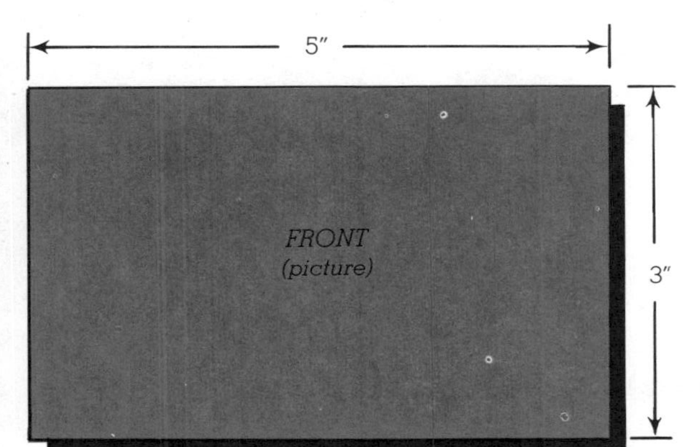

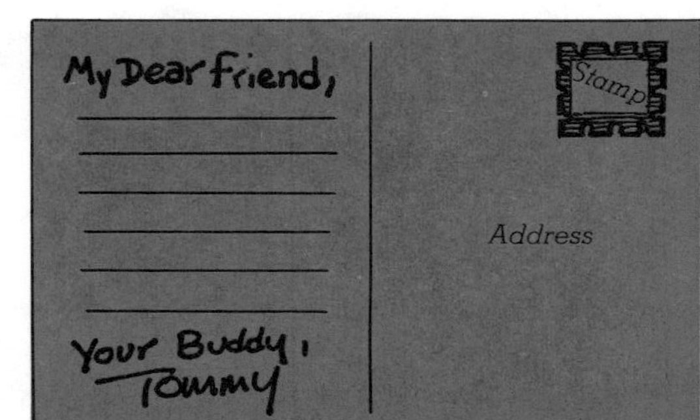

OCTOBER POEM

Oct. 15 is "World Poetry Day." Celebrate by sharing a poem. You might try writing a poem about October, fall, nature, or Halloween.

Here's a poem that may give you some ideas.

OCTOBER NIGHT

White frost comes
  and summer is over
Though crickets chirp loud
  In the brown dry clover.

Black frost comes
  And winter's begun
Though warm on my back
  Shines the noonday sun.

White frost, black frost,
  Which frost tonight?
The cold air is still,
  The cold stars are bright.

(by Agnes Louise Dean, from
The Year Around: Poems for Children)

NOVEMBER

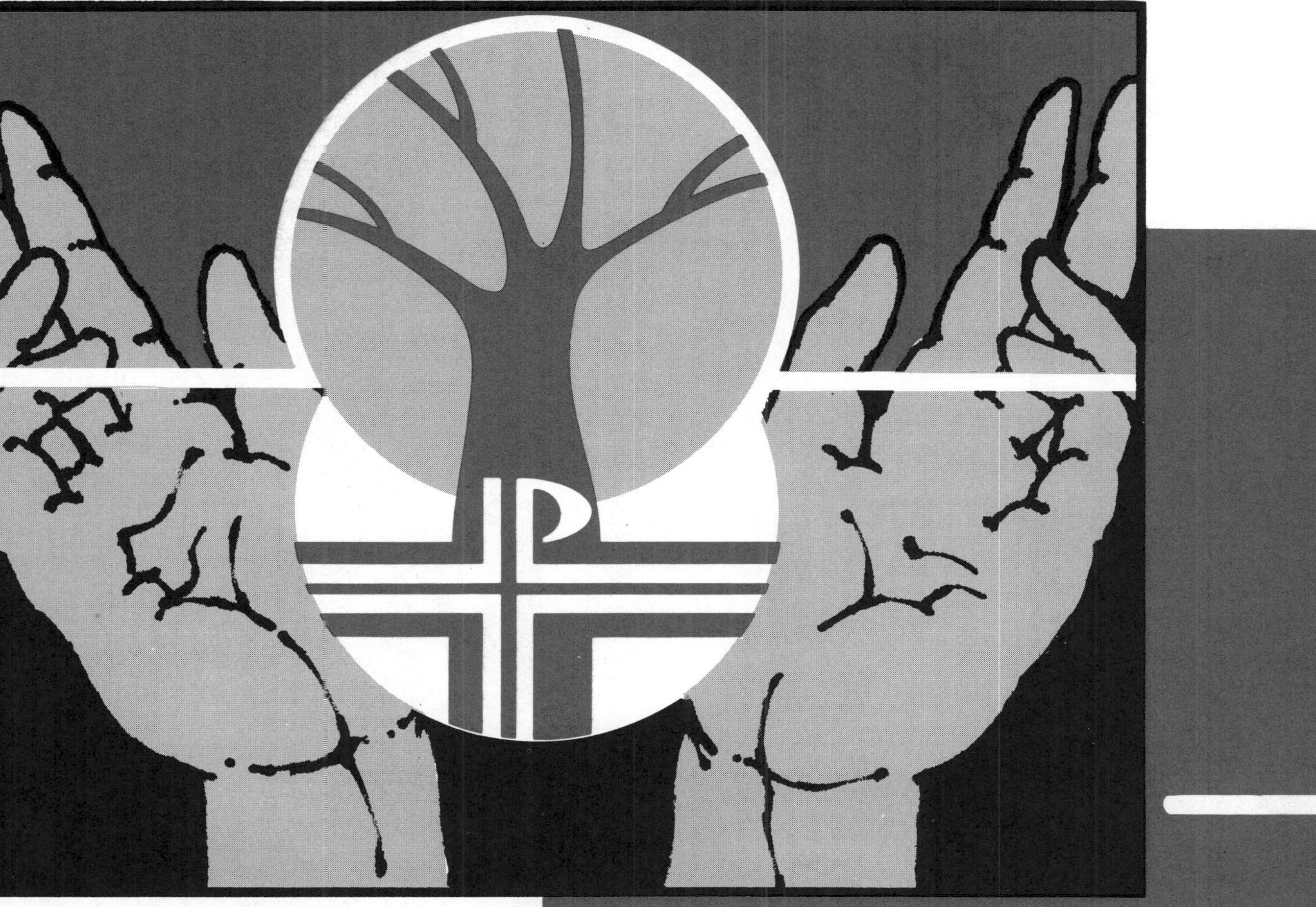

THE TWO GREAT COMMANDMENTS

NOVEMBER

BIRTHSTONE:

Topaz

A precious gem of various colors. People once believed that topaz would prevent nightmares.

FLOWER:

Chrysanthemum

This flower was once considered sacred in China, and was called "yellow glory" by Confucius.

BIRTHDATES OF PRESIDENTS/ FAMOUS PEOPLE:

James K. Polk
Born: Nov. 2, 1795

Warren G. Harding
Born: Nov. 2, 1865

James Garfield
Born: Nov. 19, 1831

Franklin Pierce
Born: Nov. 23, 1804

	1st WEEK	2nd WEEK	3rd WEEK	4thWEEK	5thWEEK
SUNDAY					
MONDAY					
TUESDAY					
WEDNESDAY					

Zachary Taylor
Born: Nov. 24, 1784

Louisa May Alcott
Born: Nov. 29, 1832

Winston Churchill
(Wartime leader and Prime Minister of England)
Born: Nov. 30, 1874

SPECIAL EVENTS:

All Saints' Day and All Souls' Day
Nov. 1 and 2

Veteran's Day
Nov. 11

Thanksgiving Day
November, fourth Thursday

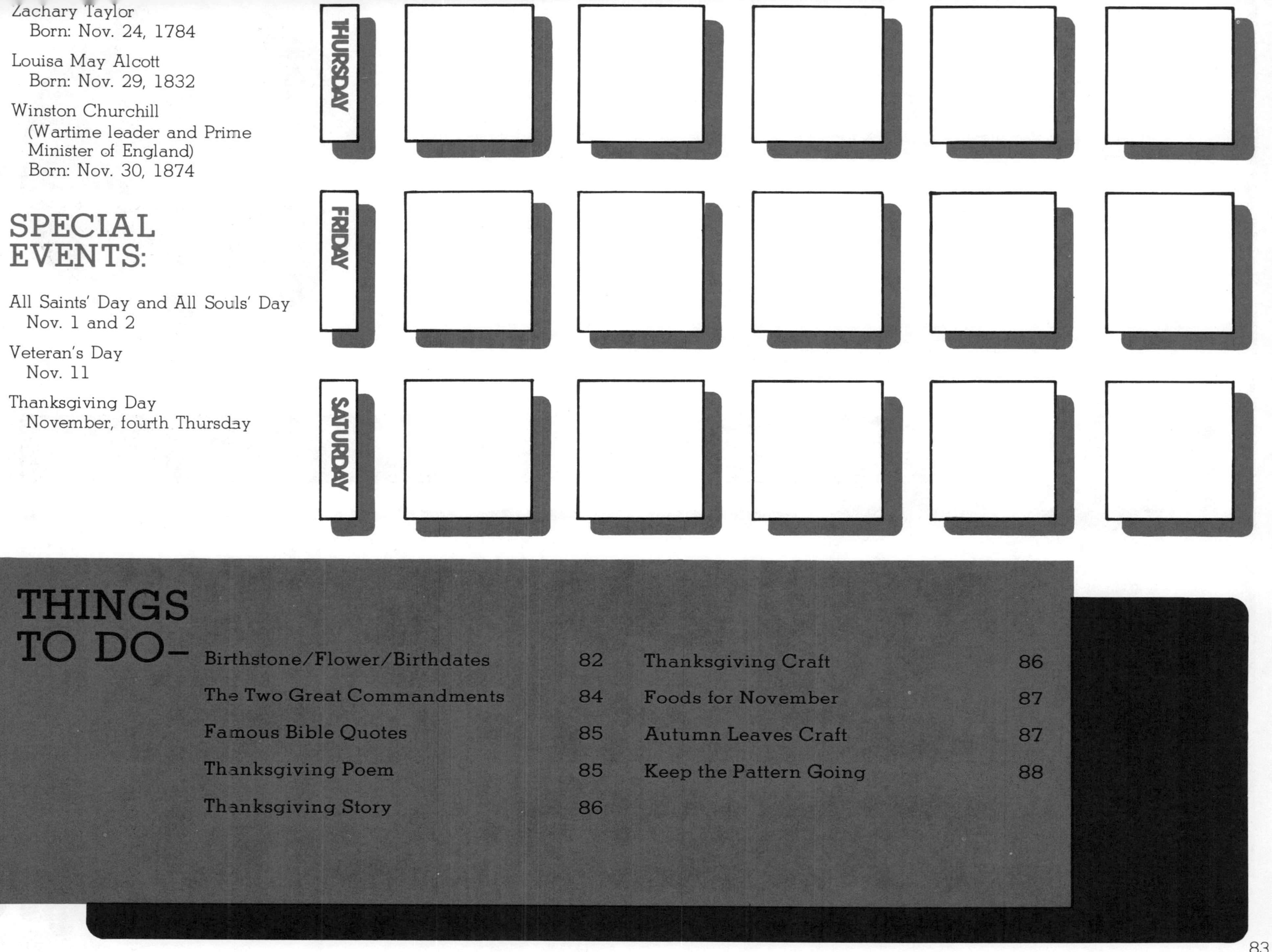

THINGS TO DO–

THE TWO GREAT COMMANDMENTS

THE TWO GREAT COMMANDMENTS

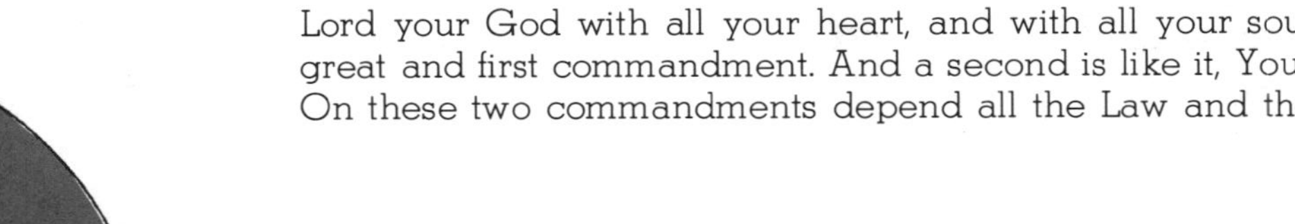

Jesus said that all the commandments could be summed up in two: "You shall love the Lord your God with all your heart, and with all your soul, and with all your mind. This is the great and first commandment. And a second is like it, You shall love your neighbor as yourself. On these two commandments depend all the Law and the prophets" *(Matthew 22:37-40)*.

THE FIRST GREAT COMMANDMENT—LOVING GOD

"You shall have no other gods before me. You shall not make for yourself a graven image, or any likeness of anything that is in heaven above, or that is on the earth beneath, or that is in the water under the earth; you shall not bow down to them or serve them; for I the Lord your God am a jealous God, visiting the iniquity of the fathers upon the children to the third and fourth generation of those who hate Me, but showing steadfast love to thousands of those who love Me and keep My commandments."

(Deuteronomy 5:7-10)

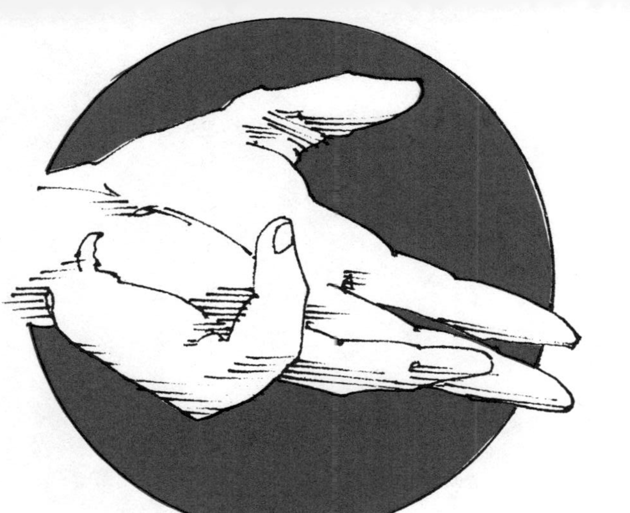

THE SECOND GREAT COMMANDMENT—LOVING OTHERS

"Honor your father and mother, as the Lord your God commanded you, that your days may be prolonged, and that it may go well with you, in the land which the Lord your God gives you. You shall not kill. Neither shall you commit adultery. Neither shall you bear false witness against your neighbor. Neither shall you covet your neighbor's wife; and you shall not desire your neighbor's house, his field, or his manservant, or his maidservant, his ox, or his ass, or anything that is your neighbor's."

(Deuteronomy 5:16-21)

"He who oppresses a poor man insults his Maker, but he who is kind to the needy honors Him."

(Proverbs 14:29-31)

FAMOUS BIBLE QUOTES

Many Bible verses have become famous. You can select some famous quotes and make them into a book.

THE GOLDEN RULE:

"You shall love your neighbor as yourself."

(Romans 13:9b).

TIME:

"For everything there is a season and a time for every matter under heaven: a time to be born, and a time to die."

(Ecclesiastes 3:1-9)

SALVATION:

"For God so loved the world that He gave His only Son, that whoever believes in Him should not perish but have eternal life."

(John 3:16)

Make these quotes into a small book; or write/print/type each one on a sheet of paper and mount the paper on plywood to make a plaque.

If you make them into a small book, make a cover page—"Famous Bible Quotes: Guides to Daily Action"—and fasten the pages with brass two-pronged fasteners. If you make plaques, put a small nail hole in the top of each plaque so you can hang it on the wall.

THANKSGIVING POEM

This is a lovely Thanksgiving poem. You may want to recite it (or read it) as a prayer at your Thanksgiving dinner.

BLESSING OVER FOOD

Blest be God
  Who did create
Porridge with milk,
  A whole full plate;
And after porridge
  Also an orange.

O, thanks to Him
  From whom they come!
Blest be He
  And blest His name!

by H.N. Bialik, from *The Year Around: Poems for Children,* 1956, Abingdon Press.

THANKSGIVING STORY

The early American settlers are credited with holding the first Thanksgiving Day in 1621, to give thanks to God for their harvests and for their well-being. George Washington proclaimed Thanksgiving as a national holiday in 1789, but it was only occasionally observed after that.

THANKSGIVING CRAFT

TURKEY PLACE CARDS

Here's what you do:

a) Collect some pine cones;

b) Draw a turkey's neck and head on drawing paper, making a long, narrow neck that curves into the head and beak; and cut it out;

c) Trace the design on red construction paper—twice for each turkey, side by side;

d) Paste them together in pairs, leaving an opening at the bottom;

e) Turn the cone on its side so that the rosette bottom of the cone is the turkey's tail;

f) Put a little glue into the open end of the paper neck and pull it over one of the forward petals of the cone;

g) Glue a small seed on each side of the head for an eye.

Pine cone

You can make as many turkeys as you have places at Thanksgiving dinner. Put a name on each turkey and put one turkey in front of each plate.

In 1827 Mrs. Sarah Hale, an editor, began to urge the national celebration of Thanksgiving. She used this text from the Bible:

> "Then he said to them, 'Go your way and eat the fat and drink sweet wine and send portions to him for whom nothing is prepared; for this day is holy to our Lord; and do not be grieved, for the joy of the Lord is your strength.'"
>
> *(Nehemiah 8:10)*

Even so, it was not until President Abraham Lincoln issued a special proclamation in 1863 that Thanksgiving became a national, as well as a religious, holiday.

Think of the many things you can be thankful for and write them down; talk to your mother, father, brothers, and sisters about these things and find out what they are thankful for.

FOODS FOR NOVEMBER

Mincemeat pies are a favorite for Thanksgiving dinner. Actually, there is no such meat as "mince." The word refers to chopped-up (minced) currants, cherries, raisins, orange and lemon peels, nuts, and meat.

Help your mother or father prepare for the Thanksgiving meal by making a mincemeat pie. You can buy prepared mincemeat; just follow the easy directions. (If you prefer, you can get all the ingredients and "mince" them yourself, and then make the pie.)

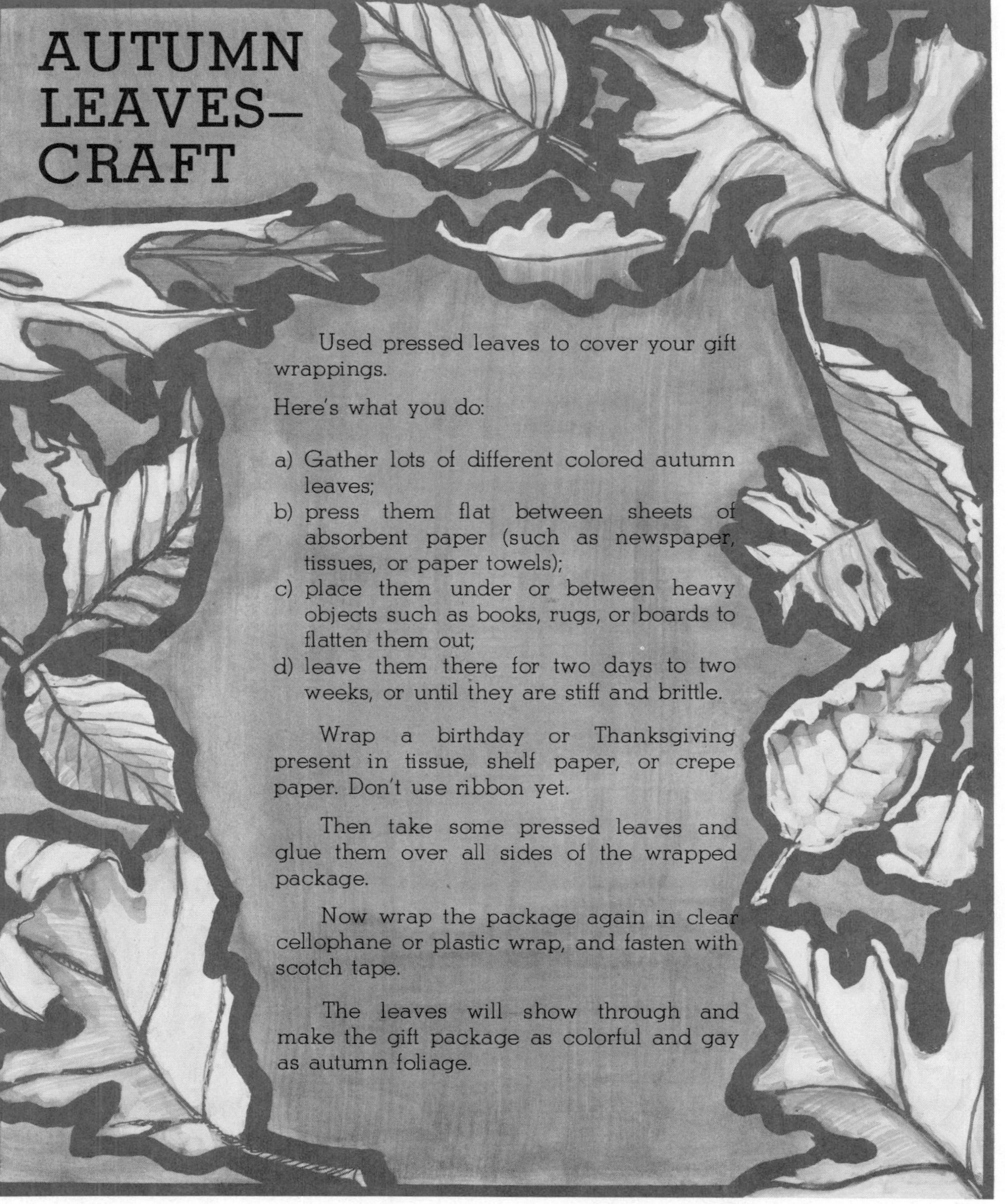

AUTUMN LEAVES—CRAFT

Used pressed leaves to cover your gift wrappings.

Here's what you do:

a) Gather lots of different colored autumn leaves;
b) press them flat between sheets of absorbent paper (such as newspaper, tissues, or paper towels);
c) place them under or between heavy objects such as books, rugs, or boards to flatten them out;
d) leave them there for two days to two weeks, or until they are stiff and brittle.

Wrap a birthday or Thanksgiving present in tissue, shelf paper, or crepe paper. Don't use ribbon yet.

Then take some pressed leaves and glue them over all sides of the wrapped package.

Now wrap the package again in clear cellophane or plastic wrap, and fasten with scotch tape.

The leaves will show through and make the gift package as colorful and gay as autumn foliage.

KEEP THE PATTERN GOING

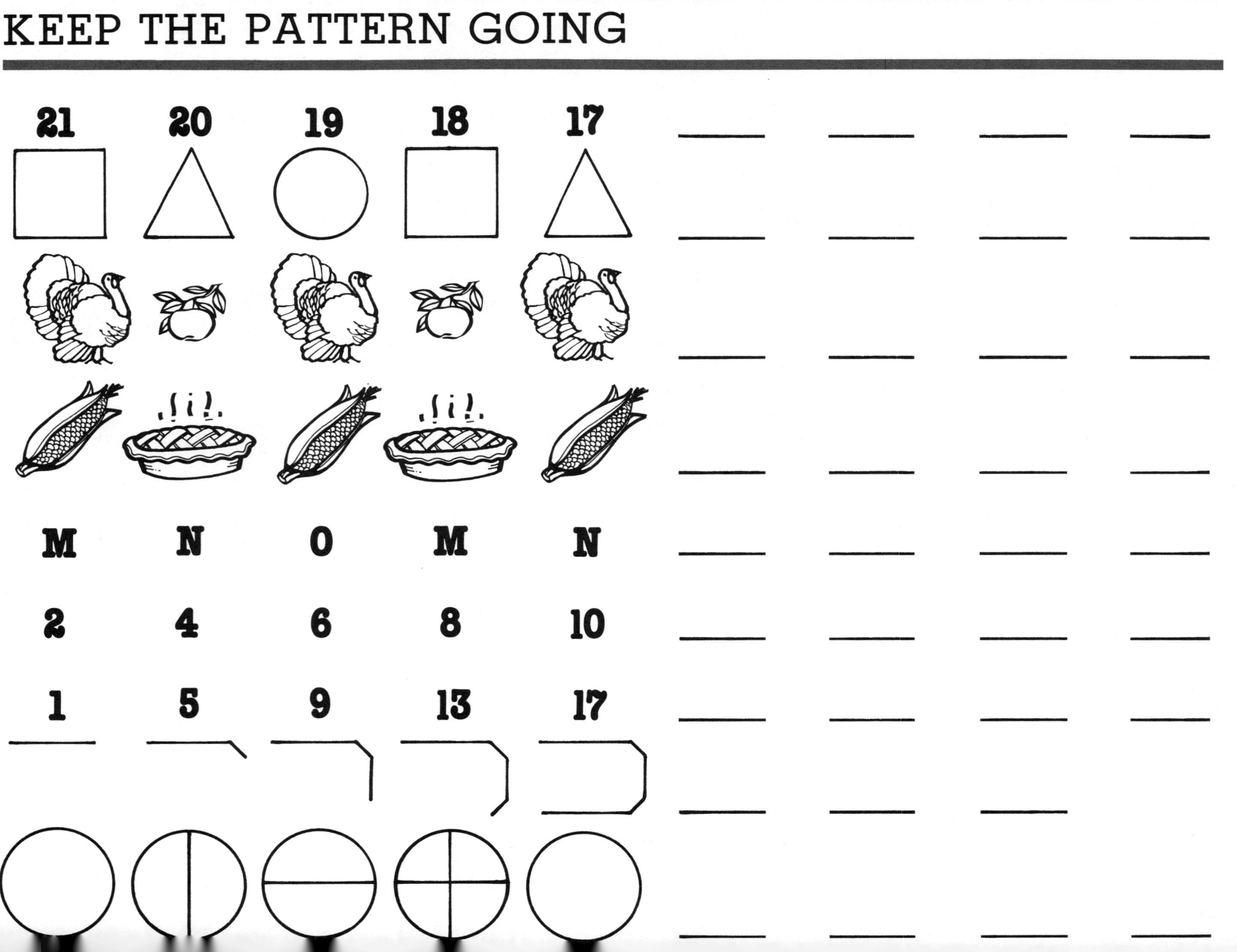

DECEMBER

PREPARING FOR CHRISTMAS

DECEMBER

	1st WEEK	2nd WEEK	3rd WEEK	4th WEEK	5th WEEK
SUNDAY					
MONDAY					
TUESDAY					
WEDNESDAY					

BIRTHSTONE:

Turquoise

FLOWER:

Narcissus

BIRTHDATES OF PRESIDENTS/ FAMOUS PEOPLE:

Martin Van Buren
Born: Dec. 5, 1782

Woodrow Wilson
Born: Dec. 28, 1856

Andrew Johnson
Born: Dec. 29, 1808

Willa Cather
(Writer)
Born: Dec. 7, 1873

John Milton
(Poet)
Born: Dec. 9, 1608

Emily Dickinson
(Poet)
Born: Dec. 10, 1830

Clara Barton
(Red Cross nurse)
Born: Dec. 12, 1821

Ludwig Van Beethoven
(Composer)
Born: Dec. 16, 1770

WHAT IS CHRISTMAS?

Christmas is Christ's birthday, the most joyous feast of the year. For many years after Christ's birth there was no Christmas celebration as we know it today. As time has passed Christmas has been celebrated not only as Christ's birthday but a time for general rejoicing, exchanging gifts, and wishing others well. Decorations include evergreens, the symbol of eternal life. Today we "deck the halls with boughs of holly" in song and in spirit.

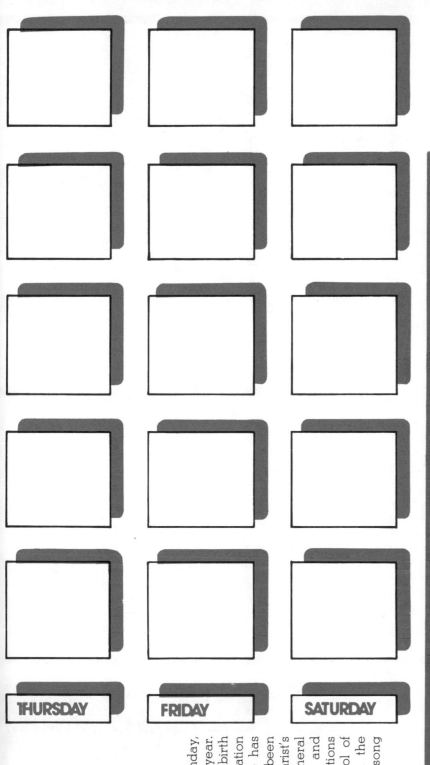

THURSDAY

FRIDAY

SATURDAY

THINGS TO DO–

PREPARING FOR CHRISTMAS

MAKE YOUR OWN MINIATURE CHRISTMAS TREE

THE CHRISTMAS STORY

"And Joseph also went up from Galilee, from the city of Nazareth, to Judea, the city of David, which is called Bethlehem, because he was of the house and lineage of David, to be enrolled with Mary his betrothed, who was with child.

And while they were there, the time came for her to be delivered. And she gave birth to her first-born son and wrapped Him in swaddling cloths, and laid Him in a manger, because there was no place for them in the inn.

And in that region there were shepherds out in the field, keeping watch over their flock by night. And an angel of the Lord appeared to them, and the glory of the Lord shone around them, and they were filled with fear. And the angel said to them, 'Be not afraid; for behold, I bring you good news of a great joy which will come to all the people; for to you is born this day in the city of David a Savior, who is Christ the Lord. And this will be a sign for you: you will find a babe wrapped in swaddling cloths and lying in a manger.'

And suddenly there was with the angel a multitude of the heavenly host praising God and saying, 'Glory to God in the highest, and on earth peace among men with whom He is pleased!'

When the angels went away from them into heaven, the shepherds said to one another, 'Let us go over to Bethlehem and see this thing that has happened, which the Lord has made known to us.' And they went with haste, and found Mary and Joseph, and the Babe lying in a manger.

And when they saw it they made known the saying which had been told them concerning this Child; and all who heard it wondered at what the shepherds told them. But Mary kept all these things, pondering them in her heart. And the shepherds returned, glorifying and praising God for all they had heard and seen, as it had been told them."

(Luke 2:4-20)

Take a branch from a dead tree; peel off leaves and bark, but leave on small branches. Paint the whole tree white. Anchor it in a bag or bucket of rocks or sand. Hang lights or decorations of your own making on it. It's a contribution you can make to your family's happiness and appreciation of the season. Call this your original Christmas tree.

The parents of Jesus were very poor, His home was bare and simple, His bed was a manger. But angels nevertheless sang songs of praise to celebrate Jesus' birth.

A beautiful and popular carol is based on their song: "Glory to God in the Highest." You may hear that carol now at Christmas time.

The first Christians did not celebrate Christmas by gathering around a Christmas tree, as we do today; yet they surely had the spirit of love and giving—which is the Spirit of Christmas.

ANIMALS AT THE MANGER

Which of the following animals would you have found at the manger where Christ was born?

donkey, fish, camel, sheep,
rhinoceros, turtle, giraffe.

Did you know that there are animal superstitions concerning Christmas? Some believe that cattle can talk on Christmas Day. And that people born between 11:00 and 12:00 on Christmas Eve can understand what the cattle say.

Answer: *donkey, camel, sheep.*

CHRISTMAS PUZZLE

1. In which section is the angel? ____, ____.
2. In which section is the star? ____, ____.
3. In which section are the Wise Men? ____, ____.
4. Make a donkey on which Mary rode in A, 5.
5. Make a Bible in B, 8.
6. Make a picture of the Baby Jesus in C, 4.
7. Make a shepherd in D, 1.

CHRISTMAS CODE I

See if you can break the code and find out the name of a famous Christmas carol.

A	B	C	D	E	F	G	H	I	J	K	L	M	N	O	P	Q	R	S	T	U	V	W	X	Y	Z
Z	—	l	÷	5	9	☆	中	!	↑	♡	$	4	◇	%	8	∞	3	#	×	ꕤ	Ø	2	△	↓	※

1. #!$5◇× ◇!☆中× 中%$↓◇!☆中×

2. Z$$!# lZ$4 Z$$!# —3!☆中×

3. 3%ꕤ◇÷ ↓%◇ Ø!3☆!◇ 4%×中53Z◇÷
   l中!$÷

4. 中%$↓ !◇9Z◇× #% ×5◇÷53Z◇÷ 4!$÷

5. #$558 !◇ 中5ZØ5◇$↓ 85Zl5 #$558
   !◇ 中5ZØ5◇$↓ 85Zl5

CHRISTMAS CODE II

See if you can break the code and find out the name of another famous Christmas carol.

A	B	C	D	E	F	G	H	I	J	K	L	M	N	O	P	Q	R	S	T	U	V	W	X	Y	Z
Z	—	l	÷	5	9	☆	中	!	↑	♡	$	4	◇	%	8	∞	3	#	×	ꕤ	Ø	2	△	↓	※

1. 25 ×中355 ♡!◇☆# %9 %3!5◇× Z35

2. —5Z3!◇☆ ☆!9×# 25 ×3ZØ5$ Z9Z3

SOAP SCULPTURE

CHRISTMAS DECORATIONS

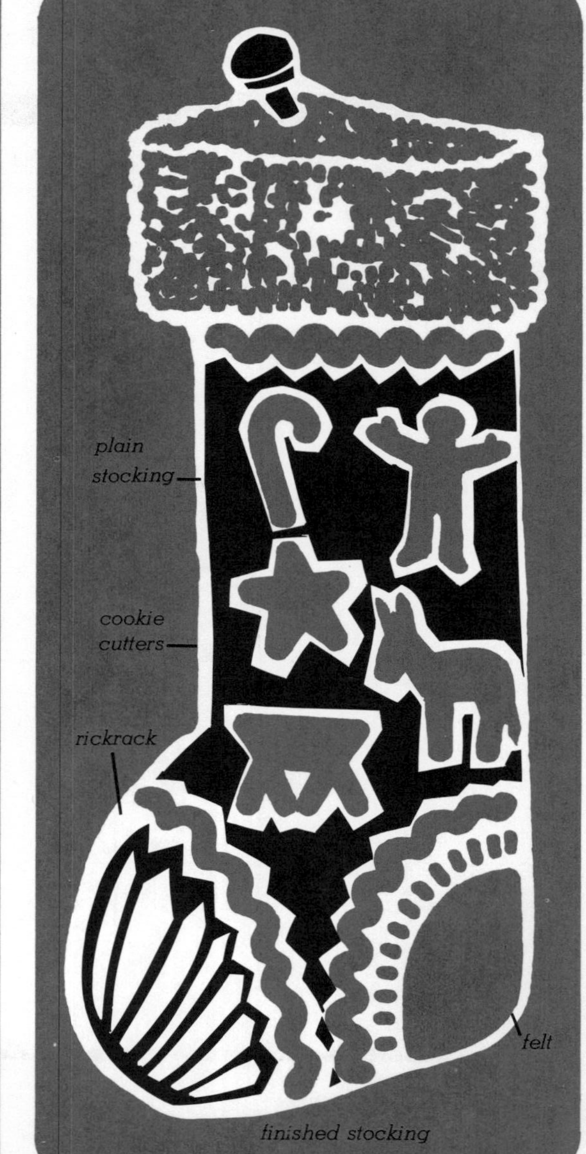

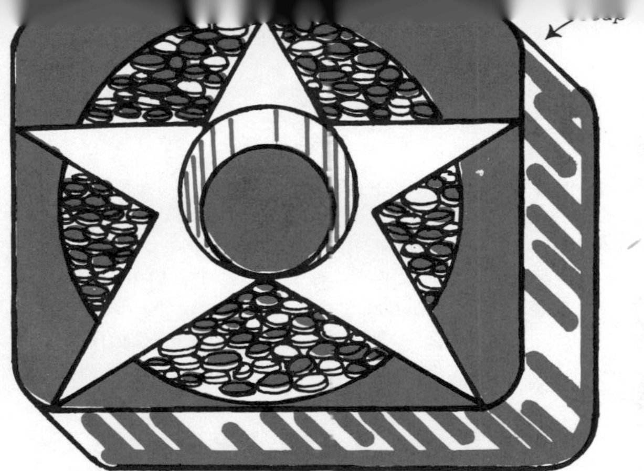

Make a soap sculpture to use in your home during the holidays.

MATERIALS NEEDED:
soap, pencil, and a kitchen knife.

Take a bar of soap and draw on a Star of Bethlehem. Carve off the extra soap. Working slowly with small bits peeled off will make it easier. You can decorate with sequins or something from your own imagination.

MYSTERY SQUARE OF WORDS AND LETTERS

See how many of the following words you can find. They are written forward, backward, and upside-down.

1. holly
2. angel
3. Bible
4. Scripture
5. Christmas
6. mistletoe
7. Holy
8. Jesus
9. Wise Men
10. manger

S	R	C	Q	W	K	F	H	J	D	L	W
B	F	H	O	L	L	Y	J	M	V	Z	I
I	H	R	S	A	A	N	G	E	L	T	S
B	F	I	R	E	K	B	C	T	U	I	E
L	K	S	C	R	I	P	T	U	R	E	M
E	O	T	E	L	T	S	I	M	Z	F	E
P	R	M	W	E	C	B	M	K	Q	Y	N
G	M	A	N	G	E	R	O	K	G	L	Z
R	G	S	V	N	G	H	J	I	U	O	T
R	Y	I	O	V	N	D	M	L	S	H	A
J	S	W	O	P	J	E	S	U	S	E	N
K	L	M	E	R	G	U	Z	X	C	R	I

Make Your Own Christmas Stocking

MATERIALS NEEDED:

felt, glue, scissors, cookie cutters, and a pen. Optional: sequins, braid, or rickrack.

Choose a few different cookie cutters, such as a Christmas tree, star of Bethlehem, or an Advent wreath. Trace them onto a piece of colored felt. Cut out and glue onto an undecorated felt stocking. Decorate with sequins or rickrack. You might donate your Christmas stocking to a church bazaar.

FOLLOW THE LETTERS
(WHAT STAR IS THIS?)

Follow the letters to discover what this picture is.

What star is this?

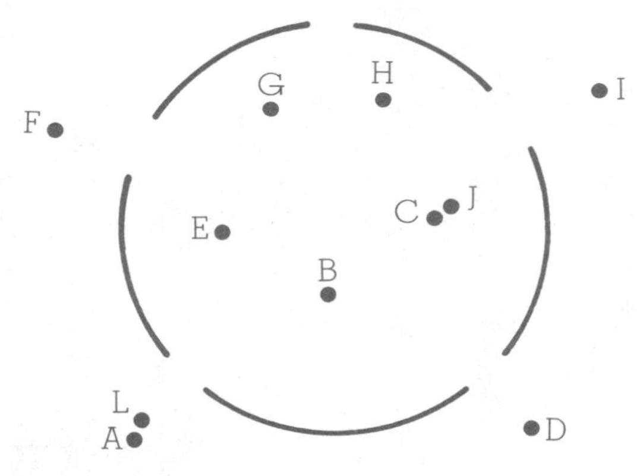

(**Answer**: the star of Bethlehem)

ST. NICHOLAS

Old Saint Nicholas is not a make-believe creature, but was a real person. Actually, St. Nicholas was a bishop who lived in Asia Minor during the fourth century A.D.; he was famous for his generosity. He is supposed to have inquired whether children had behaved well or badly; he then gave presents for the good children, a practice some parents follow even today.

He died on Dec. 6, which is now celebrated as the feast day of St. Nicholas.

CHRISTMAS EVE POEM

On a winter night
When the moon is low
The rabbits hop on the frozen snow.
The woodpecker sleeps
    in his hole in the tree
And fast asleep is the chickadee.

Twelve o'clock
And the world is still
As the Christmas star comes over the hill.
The angels sing, and sing again:
"Peace on earth, goodwill to men."

—*Marion Edey*

The Year Around: Poems for Children
Selected by Alice I. Hazeltine and Elva S. Smith.
Abingdon Press, N.Y., 1956.

MAKE A SHEPHERD

"And there were in the same country shepherds abiding in the fields, keeping watch over their flock by night."

(Luke 2:8)

MATERIALS NEEDED:

Cylinder-shaped box (like a salt or oatmeal box); material such as burlap; styrofoam ball; string; cotton; bright material; and wire.

1. Cover the cylinder-shaped box with the burlap material.
2. Glue the styrofoam ball to the top for a head.
3. Draw a face on the styrofoam ball and glue on cotton for a beard.
4. Using some of the bright material, make a head shawl by cutting a square and attaching it to the head by tying the string around it.
5. Using the remainder of the bright material, make a cloak and drape it around the figure. Glue it in several places.
6. Make a crook out of wire by bending it slightly at the top. Glue it onto the side of the shepherd.